ROUTLEDGE LIBRARY EDITIONS:
BANKING & FINANCE

INNOVATIONS IN BANKING

INNOVATIONS IN BANKING
Business Strategies and Employee Relations

TIMOTHY MORRIS

Volume 22

Routledge
Taylor & Francis Group
LONDON AND NEW YORK

First published in 1986

This edition first published in 2012
by Routledge
2 Park Square, Milton Park, Abingdon, Oxon, OX14 4RN

Simultaneously published in the USA and Canada
by Routledge
711 Third Avenue, New York, NY 10017

Routledge is an imprint of the Taylor & Francis Group, an informa business

British Library Cataloguing in Publication Data
A catalogue record for this book is available from the British Library

ISBN: 978-0-415-52086-7 (Set)
eISBN: 978-0-203-10819-2 (Set)
ISBN: 978-0-415-52667-8 (Volume 22)
eISBN: 978-0-203-11687-6 (Volume 22)

Publisher's Note
The publisher has gone to great lengths to ensure the quality of this reprint but points out that some imperfections in the original copies may be apparent.

Disclaimer
The publisher has made every effort to trace copyright holders and would welcome correspondence from those they have been unable to trace.

MIX
Paper from
responsible sources
FSC® C013604

INNOVATIONS in BANKING

Business Strategies and Employee Relations

TIMOTHY MORRIS

CROOM HELM
London • Sydney • Wolfeboro, New Hampshire

Croom Helm Ltd, Provident House, Burrell Row,
Beckenham, Kent BR3 1AT
Croom Helm Australia Pty Ltd, Suite 4, 6th Floor,
64-76 Kippax Street, Surry Hills, NSW 2010, Australia

British Library Cataloguing in Publication Data

Morris, Timothy
Innovations in banking: business strategies and employee relations.
1. Banks and banking — England — History — 20th Century 2. Industrial relations — England — History — 20th Century
I. Title
331'.0413321'0942 HD6976.B262G7

ISBN 0-7099-4607-4

Croom Helm, 27 South Main Street
Wolfeboro, New Hampshire
03894-2069

Library of Congress Cataloging-in-Publication Data

Morris, Timothy, 1953-
Innovations in banking.

"Loosely derived from my Ph. D. thesis" – Pref.
Bibliography: p.
Includes index.
1. Bank management – Great Britain. 2. Trade-unions – Bank employees – Great Britain. 3. Banks and banking – Great Britain – Personnel management. 4. Industrial relations – Great Britain. I. Title.
HG2988.M675 1986 332.1'068'3 86-13400

CONTENTS

TABLES AND FIGURES

Tables

Figures

PREFACE

This book is loosely derived from my PhD thesis, which was a study of inter-union competition in the banks. I am grateful to the ESRC for financial support which enabled me to undertake the research as a student at the London School of Economics, and to the London Business School for providing me with a Research Fellowship which enabled me to complete the writing of the book.

Both book and thesis have drawn on the knowledge and interest shown by a number of managers and union officials. The interviews I conducted with these people invariably lasted at least an hour and I am grateful for the time they gave me. In addition, I have particularly benefited from extended discussions and comments on drafts from Nick Cowan and John Waine of FLCBE, from Christine Allen of the CBU and Jon Robinson and Steve Gamble of BIFU.

Various colleagues and friends are owed my thanks for help in completing this book. In particular, David Marsden and Paul Willman have given great support and perceptive analysis for which I am indebted. I have also benefited from discussions with Tom Johnston, Ben Roberts, Barbara Townley and Stephen Wood. Thanks are due to Gaynor Kim-Sing, Lucille Bailey and Kate Chalk and last but not least to Dee McQuillan. The usual disclaimers regarding the text apply, and I accept sole responsibility for errors or inaccuracies therein.

1 INTRODUCTION

Over the last 20 years or so much work has inevitably focused on the relationship between British labour relations and poor economic performance. The usual approach has been to concentrate on certain features of economic decline, either by case study or general survey work and examine the degree of coincidence with labour relations features; hence the overwhelming perspective has been one of labour relations as a problem, or at least a significant contributory factor, to relative failure (Batstone, 1984, chap. 4). In contrast, the focus here is on what may be seen as a relatively successful industry both in economic and labour management terms. The intention is thus to explore this success and the extent to which labour relations have contributed, or more negatively, not inhibited it.

This begs the question of how success is measured? If the criteria of financial performance are used, it is arguable that the major English clearing banks (see Table 1.1) have, during much of the post-war period, experienced consistent profitability and growth, domestically and abroad. Of course, in real terms the return on assets employed may show a more cyclical trend, and the banks have argued that despite the enormous size of their profits in absolute terms, their margins have recently been below those enjoyed in the earlier boom periods of, say, the early 1970s (CLCB, 1981). The large absolute profit figures are said to distort true comparisons with other sectors of the economy where, at least more recently, the banks argue that margins are stronger (Bevan, 1985). None the less, the clearers have not suffered so greatly from the loss of markets through foreign competition which has been at the heart of Britain's economic decline in some sectors of manufacturing industry and have remained more consistently profitable. Indeed their methods and policies have even been blamed for some of the failures of British industry elsewhere (see Wilson Committee Report, 1981; Bis, 1981a). In the narrow economic terms this profitable growth is at the heart of the criteria of 'success'.

This is not to claim that management in the banks must be superior. Their performance has been assisted by external factors such as the high interest rate policies adopted to contain inflation over the past decade, and by the general shift away from cash and towards the use of bank accounts which has provided considerable scope for volume growth.

Table 1.1: Major English Clearing Banks

1967	1980	1986
Barclays	Barclays	Barclays
Midland	National Westminster	National Westminster
Lloyds	Midland	Midland
Westminster	Lloyds	Lloyds
National Provincial	Williams & Glyn's	
Martins		
District		
Williams Deacon		
Glyn, Mills		
Coutts		
National		

Note: Ranked by asset size.

Moreover, the monopoly of the clearing system for cheques and credits placed them in a strong position *vis-à-vis* any potential competitors for many years. On the other hand, the clearing banks might claim that sound management has enabled them to develop new products, manage growth while containing costs by ambitious programmes of technical investment over the last 25 years, and by and large, through prudent system of reporting and control, not be caught out by some of the more speculative areas of lending which have ended in disaster, notably the secondary banking crisis of the mid-1970s. But bad debts do exist and remain a contemporary problem of potentially large proportions. Overall, though, it is not the contention of this book that success is solely explained by management competence either financially or in terms of labour strategies.

Measuring success in labour management terms is also fraught with problems. If the banks have been blessed with a relatively co-operative workforce this, in the view of some of their critics, is in spite of rather than because of their management skills. None the less, one of the themes developed below is that labour relations have been crucial in enabling the banks to manage growth profitably. Expressed negatively, it could be said that from the employers' point of view, successful labour management has meant the general record of co-operation with little industrial action and the absence of marked resistance to the processes of technical change or to issues of managerial prerogative in the area of work organisation. This pattern has, in turn, contributed to the success of the banks' business strategies in so far as they have been able to raise labour productivity markedly, and to provide a reliable and continuous service to their customers.

As white-collar employers with a majority of young female staff occupying the junior grades, this may not be considered exceptional. White-collar workers have generally been seen to identify more closely with managerial values (Hyman and Price, 1983) and be less likely to establish the sorts of job controls around which powerful shopfloor resistance developed (Batstone *et al.* 1977). The co-operation of bank clerks might thus be explained by reference to general values of white-collar workers (Prandy *et al.* 1982), by their structural 'ambivalence' within the capitalist system between managers and workers (Crompton, 1976), or by reference to workforce characteristics and their division into small work establishments (the average branch size is still under 15 people) which offset any alienating effects of the largeness of the banks overall (Bain, 1970). It may also be explained by reference to the managerial control strategy exerted through the internal promotion systems. Edwards (1979) has termed this 'bureaucratic' control and argued that it buttresses managerial authority by raising the costs to the individual employee of opposition in terms of jeopardising career prospects.

Nevertheless, the record in the banks and finance sector more generally has been one of exceptional co-operation. One result was that they remained largely insulated from the spread of strike action in the 1970s into other white-collar areas (P. Edwards, 1983). Moreover, bank staff have tended to prefer representation in staff associations, a form of union which has generally been seen (or criticised) as employer-dominated, and thus powerless (Blackburn, 1967; Allen and Williams, 1960). Staff associations in fact exist in other sectors, including manufacturing, but are most common in the finance sector and within the latter have been established longest in the clearing banks (Certification Officer, 1979). As is argued below, they reflect the exceptionally co-operative employment relationship and contribute towards it in the way in which they have responded to management policies.

In summary, then, the banks are somewhat exceptional in having a long record of profitability and growth in the post-war period. Underpinning this, their labour relations have been characterised as non-conflictual, with a high degree of managerial prerogative remaining intact while elsewhere in British industry shopfloor control was advancing. The absence of resistance to change has enabled the banks to introduce substantial innovations to work processes which, *inter alia,* raised efficiency and enabled them to cope with a growing customer market. In the context of increasing product market competition and the drive for increased efficiency to manage growth profitability, the book examines how the banks have been able to sustain their co-operative labour relations and thus to effect change without significant resistance. It looks at the content of the strategies they adopted and the processes of implementing them, and tries to evaluate to what extent they contributed to the banks' corporate success. Allied to this, the book explores how the banks managed the inter-union rivalary to their advantage and reconciled the introduction of joint negotiation with the pursuit of efficient growth during a period of exceptional wage inflation.

Management of Employee Relations

In taking as its subject area the management of employee relations, this book contributes to the growing literature in this area both of survey and case-study analysis (see for example, Batstone *et al.*, 1984; Willman and Winch, 1985). It can be argued that this focus is both a reaction to previous academic preoccupations with trade union behaviour and with a recognition that management activity was highly, if not primarily, important for the nature of industrial relations in the enterprise (Clegg, 1976; Purcell, 1983; Kochan *et al.*, 1984). In banking, this may be especially so, because another important determinant — the role of the trade unions — has been moderated by the relatively compliant attitudes of their members to managerial control. None the less, in what follows it is stressed that a third 'actor', the state, or government and its agencies, has been exceptionally influential; this is partly because the banks are very large employers and assumed to influence the general level of wages in the economy, so that governments of both major parties have seen fit to intervene on pay, trade union relationships and recognition. It is also explained by the quasi-public position the banks have in the distribution of money and the implementation of economic policy which has required a close supervisory role by the monetary authorities (the Treasury and Bank of England). In effect this confirms Ferner's (1985) argument that a 'political contingency' may operate in the private sector and significantly mediate management autonomy.

Secondly, the analysis concentrates on strategic decisions, in the sense developed by Chandler (1962) of strategy as 'the determination of the basic long-term goals and objectives of an enterprise and adaptation of courses of action and the allocation of resources necessary for carrying out these goals'. Chandler and other management theorists have usually seen strategies as primarily concerned with corporate decisions concerning market position, pricing and product portfolio. If it is assumed labour strategies are essentially concerned with trade union relations then they are less likely to be articulated so clearly, not least because senior management spends relatively little time on the subject, except in times of crises (Purcell, 1983; Hickson and Mallory, 1981). However as Timperley (1980) has argued, senior management will still have an impact on labour relations decisions in so far as they shape the contexts or parameters in which these are taken by prior policy-making on the central business areas. Furthermore, if employee relations is taken in a broader sense to mean 'the management of the human resource' in the process of organisational change, then it is evident that many issues, including management development, levels of productivity, motivation, the introduction of technological changes and the rewards system and structure, are the subject of senior management's attention (Pettigrew, 1985). It is in this broader sense that employee relations has been used in this book.

Nevertheless, the term strategy has been used with different meanings and remains a problematic concept in some ways (Mintzberg, 1978; Thurley and Wood, 1983). That managers work with long-term coherent plans designed to achieve predetermined goals does make many assumptions about the realities of organisational behaviour and the dynamics of managerial action: strategies may exist as corporate level blueprints, for instance, but their effective implementation may be mediated by factors including intra-organisational conflict, obstacles such as union or work-group resistance, or differing local conditions such as labour market variations. The analytical use of strategy therefore predictably involves a top-down of change and one which understates the problems and significance of implementation and local improvisations. Indeed it may be that an *a priori* assumption of strategy is unjustifiable, in so far as it imputes a rationality to decision-making which needs to be demonstrated empirically.

In the banks, however, it is arguable that such an approach to analysing the management of labour is justifiable and particularly relevant for a number of reasons. The first concerns the centralised nature of management control, so that only the minimum of local autonomy either over procedural issues or substantive matters such as pay, conditions of employment, the organisation of work and career patterns has traditionally been allowed. Associated with this centralised control is the emphasis on formalised modes of decision-making through committees of the banks' executives — their general managers, who are responsible for an operating division or support function. In effect, therefore, decision-making is bureaucratic and there is an overlap between the functions of policy-making and policy execution in practice. Secondly, all the banks have favoured general management skills and development, so that autonomous and powerful personnel functions with independent values or interests have not typically emerged (Legge, 1978). Personnel management has remained integrated relatively unproblematically within the business, by specialising primarily in the broad development of a managerial cadre, training, recruiting and manpower planning. Usually, the heads of the personnel function in the banks have not been personnel 'professionals' but 'high-flying' bankers broadening their managerial experience for a period. Thirdly, the commercial environment has been sufficiently stable to facilitate long-term planning in all areas of management. Even as the pace of change has accelerated, the importance of planning has not diminished but is now directed towards flexibility rather than rigid forecasting. The management culture in banking has thus been very much oriented to careful and planned approaches to change although the degree to which it is possible to talk of employee relations strategies as explicitly articulated and pre-defined plans of action towards clear goals will be commented on in the concluding chapter.

Yet how far can the banks be discussed collectively? Certainly they have been seen (and criticised) as being very similar. Undoubtedly, this derives in part from similar managerial choices over growth and market strategy in the past, but homogeneity also stems from the common operational reliance on the clearing system through which each other's business could be processed and from the standard method of raising funds through retail deposits which were then lent on by the short-term overdraft (see Morse, 1981). Each clearer also developed similar systems of management through teams of general managers (Nevin and Davis, 1973) although in the 1970s more complex market strategies led to greater diversification in management organisations: Lloyds Bank appointed a group chief executive, for instance, in the early 1970s to oversee all operational decisions and its current chairman tends to be less involved in this aspect of the management, concentrating on purely strategic planning.

Broadly speaking, it can also be said that the direction of the growth strategies the banks have pursued is similar. In the 1960s each sought to expand its branch network; in the 1970s the emphasis was upon international diversification; in the 1980s each bank has diversified into other parts of the finance sector (such as the capital markets). Yet as competition has opened up, choices about marketing, about technical systems for cash distribution, corporate treasury management, about the desired shape of the branch structure and about methods of international diversification begin to vary more. In turn, having operated as a cartel in the labour market (their oligopoly product market position determining the oligopsony role in the labour market), there is evidence of a growing diversification in labour market policies, as will be shown.

The London Clearing Banks

This section describes the development of the clearing banks and their role in the context of the finance sector. It seeks to show that they play a dominant part in the sector in terms of several elements of labour relations. The nature and extent of union membership in the banks is also discussed as a precursor to the analysis of labour management in the following chapters. Finally, an outline of the structure of the rest of the book is given.

History

The clearing banks emerged in the nineteenth century as joint stock companies based around the City of London and several large provinicial cities. Originally they did not control the clearing system for cheques, but acquired this from the private banks which had started it around 1770 when taking them over (Nevin and Davis, 1970). The advantage of the clearing system was that it presented an easy means of transferring the money between the banks' customers, and thus attracted the deposits which the banks used for lending. In this process the clearing banks' role became differentiated from the other banks. They were placed under the control of the central bank, the Bank of England, which also acquired a monopoly on note issue, and they also became firmly distinguished from the merchant banks which did not rely on deposits from the public for their financing activities (Sayers, 1957). The clearing system, located in London and in regional clearing centres, presented the opportunity to spread the costs of money transmission and made the banks more attractive by extending their outlets, but it required close operational co-operation. This was formally controlled through the Committee of London Clearing Bankers (CLCB), comprising the chairmen of each of the clearers, acting effectively as the trade association of the industry and co-ordinating issues of joint concern, be they technical or commercial. The actual operations of the clearing system were overseen by the Bankers Clearing House, however, whose membership originally was limited to the clearing banks but now extends to other retail banks and, following the recent Child Report, will also be open to other financial institutions, subject to certain volume and cost criteria (D. Child, 1984).

The clearers were originally local banks which spread by merger, acquisition and natural growth, particularly around the beginning of the twentieth century. The mode of formation left its mark on the individual bank's management systems. Barclays had a much stronger tradition of decentralised control to its local directors, for example, This derived from its origins in the merger of over a dozen small regional banks in the latter part of the nineteenth century (in many cases started by Quakers), each of which tended to guard its autonomy and traditional methods long afterwards (Tuke and Gillman, 1972). The Midland, in contrast, emerging from the acquisitions of the dominant London and Midland Bank, was always more centralised and its practices more standardised. These variations did not extend to the area of labour management, however. The process of concentration was largely checked by the intervention of the authorities at the end of the First World War (Colwyn Committee Report, 1918). Further mergers would, it was feared, place too much power in the hands of the banks against the public interest. This left eleven banks which fell into two distinct groups. Those in the first group were larger and independently owned, with about 85 per cent of the total assests of the group. The second group of six comprised much smaller banks which were also in most cases wholly or partly owned by the larger ones, but operated independently.

This structure remained more or less intact until the late 1960s, when a further spate of mergers was permitted. After the signal from the Bank of England, Barclays acquired Martins Bank; the National Provincial, which also owned the District Bank, merged with the Westminster to form the National Westminster. Both of these changes took place in 1968. Coutts and Co., a wholly-owned subsidiary of the National Provincial, was also brought into the National Westminster Group but continued to operate independently, with its own seat on the CLCB. Thirdly, Williams and Glyn's Bank was formed in 1969 from the merger of three smaller banks, Glyn Mills and Co., Williams Deacon's and the National Bank. However, a fruther proposal to merge Barclays and Lloyds was disallowed, for fear of the likely duopoly which would result (Monopolies and Mergers, 1968). Thereafter these five banks operated as the London clearers until 1985, when Williams and Glyn's merged with its Scottish partner, the Royal Bank of Scotland, to form a UK clearer. This prompted a reform of the Committee of London Clearing Bankers into the Committee of London and Scottish Banks, combining the main English and Scottish clearers.

Until then, the Scottish clearers had developed in parallel, but operated independently. Banking law is different is Scotland and the rights and functions of the clearers (over note issue) are thus distinctive (Gaskin, 1974). None the less, the English clearers have held equity stakes in their Scottish counterparts for some time. The Northern Irish Banks (the Ulster Bank and the Northern Bank) are also wholly-owned subsidiaries of the National Westminster and Midland Banks respectively.

This book discusses only one (albeit the major) of the banks' activities. For they have become multi-divisional companies (see Figure 1.1) organised around a number of profit or cost centres and diversified into other areas of the finance sector since the Second World War, notably hire purchase and credit factoring, merchant banking, insurance services, credit card operations, international banking and, latterly, the securities markets by acquisition and natural growth. In this way, their interests have spread across the whole sector, but each business has tended to be run separately from the point of view of labour relations although coordinated from the centre in the general management structure and heavily influenced by what happens in the domestic banking division because of its dominant size. Table 1.2 shows the total UK staff of each bank and the proportion employed in their domestic banking divisions as at 1983.

Figure 1.1: Organisational Structure of a Clearing Bank

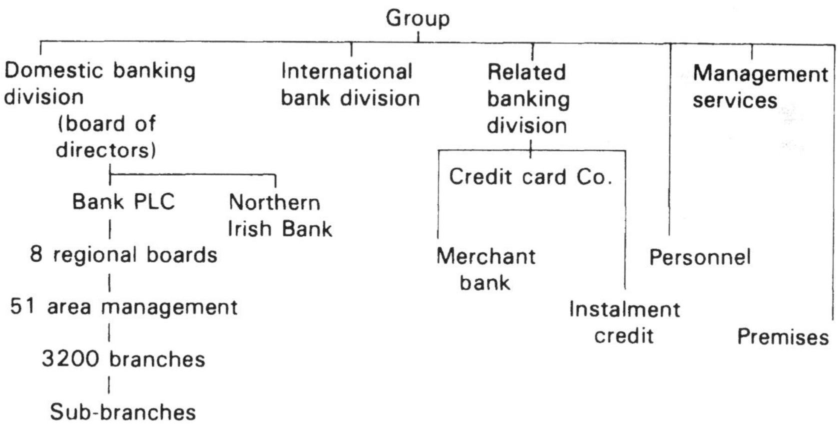

Table 1.2: Staff Numbers, 1983

	UK Banking Division	UK Total	Group Total
Barclays	61,800	75,000	121,500
Lloyds	46,100	53,100	69,800
Midland	49,300	67,900	89,500
Natwest	70,500	80,700	90,700

Source: CLCB

The London clearers are, then, part of the larger finance sector, covering wholesale money markets, foreign currency markets and trade financing, the capital markets located on the Stock Exchange, insurance and mortgage lending dominated by the building societies. This sector as a whole has grown rapidly in terms of assets employed and in employment over the last 20 years. Total employment in the sector (SIC 81–85) now exceeds 1.85 million, having risen by 387,000 since 1975. This growth stands in contrast to the contraction in employment in the primary and secondary sectors over the last 20 years, and means that 7.25 per cent of the employed labour force are in this sector.

Within the broader sector it is arguable that the clearing banks occupy a crucial position, at least in terms of employment conditions, and that their decisions have wider implications (see Table 1.3). This stems from the 'patterned' pay settlements which derive from clearing bank decisions and cover many of the foreign banks, the building societies and, less directly, the insurance companies. In the past, frequent government scrutiny of bank pay levels has been based on the assumed effect this has on other major white-collar employers, including the civil service and local government, the Bank of England and oil companies (NBPI, Report no. 6, 1965; Pay Board, 1974). Many of the other banks and the building societies have also recruited clerical staff from the clearers and to that extent they act as a training resource for the finance sector. So, apart from directly negotiating the terms of their own UK banking staff, who number 240,000, the clearers' decisions have a wider impact on the finance sector and white-collar employees in other industries.

Table 1.3: Employment in Banking

	TOTAL BANKING SECTOR	LONDON CLEARERS UK DIVISIONS
1970	253.0	173.3
1975	320.7	202.0
1979	334.0	218.7
1982	370.9	232.5
1984	384.4	238.5

Sources: De Gazette, CLCB

Outline of the Book

Although the book adopts a broadly chronological ouline, this is not meant to imply that it is a history of labour relations. Rather, it is intended to illustrate the dynamic of change and the dimensions of strategic activity: how the approach to managing labour has evolved in the context of the growing competition facing the banks. To this end, Chapter 2 examines the business environment of the banks, and the trends towards market diversification and interpenetration in the different segments of the finance sector which have eroded the oligopoly position of the clearers. It stresses the importance of technical innovations and government policies in facilitating these changes. Chapter 3 then looks at the origins and nature of the rivalry between the national trade union, now called BIFU, and the staff associations (now called staff unions) in each bank. It charts the development of the collective bargaining structure up to the end of the 1960s, showing how this dual representation was fostered by the banks' hostility to the national union. It also shows how certain crises in labour management resulted in first the introduction of domestic pay negotiation with the associations, and then subsequently the collapse of this system and its replacement by a national forum.

Chapter 4 explores the operation of national bargaining to the end of the 1970s, when procedures collapsed due to inter-union hostility. This national machinery is analysed as part of a wider employer strategy which pursued the twin aims of stability and greater efficiency and related to the dominant commercial objectives of the banks in this high growth period. Chapter 5 looks at the redirection of management objectives since then, suggesting that in the pursuit of cost control and productivity growth, there have been reforms to the strategies of the banks in the areas of pay, career paths and work organisation. This is related to the discussion of technical innovation in Chapter 6, which also looks at the implications for staffing levels and careers. It also examines the prospects for employment in the light of arguments about the position of women as the 'secondary' segment in the banks' internal labour markets. Chapter 7 then considers the response of the trade union and staff associations to this changing environment. It argues that their behaviour has to be understood in the light of their continuing competition for dominance, exploring in some detail efforts to resolve this by merger and the reasons for their failure. The chapter concludes that the firmer labour relations policies of the banks have created profound problems for both the national union and staff unions, whose policies were for long predicated upon highly co-operative strategies with the employers. In the concluding chapter, the arguments are pulled together, and some of the prospects for the future are surveyed.

2 BUSINESS STRATEGIES AND THE MANAGEMENT OF EMPLOYEE RELATIONS

This chapter examines some of the issues involved in studying the relationship between the commercial strategies which lie at the heart of corporate decision-making and the management of labour. In looking at the clearing banks it emphasises the need for a longitudinal approach which explores the evolution of managerial goals in changing contexts and market conditions. Furthermore, though, the intention is to stress that the generation of policies in the area of labour management has been influenced by certain long-standing values broadly encapsulated in the idea of a paternalistic employment relationship and has not been strictly determined by the logic of the commericial environment. Indeed, it is argued throughout that there has consistently been a dichotomy in management policies stemming from efforts to control labour costs, on the one hand, and the desire to sustain commitment and motivation on the other. These are associated with the nature of competition facing the banks. Having looked at these factors in some detail, the chapter sets the stage for an analysis of how key areas of employee relations have been managed.

Management Strategy and Objectives

Part of the greater interest in management's role has involved a recognition of the importance of business objectives in framing the shape and content of labour relations (Poole and Mansfield, 1980; Kochan *et al.*, 1984). Work emphasising the derivative nature of labour strategies and showing how the market determines management thinking and behaviour has provided a useful insight into this area.

Yet in elaborating general models of this linkage, researchers have faced the problem that the increasing heterogeneity of conditions confronting enterprises has called for individualised and particularistic business policies (Thomson, 1983). These have occurred both between enterprises and within single firms operating in numerous product markets and usually organised on a divisional basis. There are also further problems of a conceptual nature in analysing management behaviour and objectives, prompting for instance the long-standing debate on whether managers in the private sector are profit maximising or otherwise. But less has been said about the influence of differing market conditions in which firms operate and the changing dimensions of competitive pressure over a period of time (Porter, 1980), certainly in terms of how these may work through to the management of labour relations.

These factors help to explain the problems of generalising discussions of management strategies in industrial/labour relations. Often they have relied on ideal types or categories which fail fully to convey the nature of the interaction between corporate plans and the labour relations function, or to incorporate some explanation of the conditions under which this relationship changes. For example, different parts of the private service sector are grouped together by Thurley and Wood (1983) in their explication of the concept of a labour relations strategy. In so doing they are forced to overlook real differences within various parts of this sector in both market conditions and labour management, for instance in career structures or recruitment policies. Other analyses have been forced to rely on rather broad categories which fail to capture the range of variety between enterprises in such basic structural factors as the degree of centralisation in decision-making (Fox, 1974; Purcell and Sisson, 1983).

Associated with this has been the tendency in the past to see collective bargaining arrangements as coterminous with or the predominant part of a firm's industrial relations strategy (Purcell and Smith, 1979; Kinnie, 1985). Of course, despite the decline in union membership nationally, joint regulation remains an important method of determining procedural and substantive facets of employment, but such analytical frameworks are clearly more applicable to (and derived from) the manufacturing sector, where strongly organised trade unions could place a brake on managerial prerogative through the assertion of job controls. More broadly, by considering bargaining alone, the nature of the employer's labour strategy is not fully explored, for this includes a range of issues which are often not negotiable, such as the organisational structure of the enterprise and managerial reporting relationships, manpower development policies and payment systems. This is especially the case in the banks which, like other white-collar employers in the private sector, deal with weak trade unions (adopting atypical forms) and where the scope of joint regulation is limited.

Moreover the importance of enterprise values or traditions, often reflecting the origins of the firm or its founders, has tended to be downplayed or ignored. This may reflect the development of theories of organisational strategy within the 'harder' social science disciplines which have concentrated on the relationship between structural form and decision processes and outcomes. The impact of values is obviously extremely difficult to conceptualise or assess, but managers and staff themselves have often stressed the importance of company norms or styles, most notably perhaps with the Quaker firms in Britain. To an extent, this area has received more recently attention, both in studies of the management of change and in broader analyses which have seen company 'culture' as a key contributory factor to corporate performance but again less has been said about it in the area of employee relations (Peters and Waterman, 1982; Purcell, 1986).

To overcome the problem of adequately capturing the diversity in contextual factors and management policies, labour relations and organisational change have been explored more intensively at the level of the firm, or even below it (Pettigrew, 1985; Kelly, 1984). Others have looked at specific industries or trading monopolies in the public sector (Marsden *et al.*, 1985; Batstone *et al.*, 1984). These studies have tended to convey more successfully the thinking behind labour relations strategies and the influence of the commercial policies on them. They have also been able to examine more fully the processes of strategy formulation as well as the constraints upon management in implementing decisions, including political controls or organisational history and management structure (Willman and Winch, 1985). Again, though, these studies confirm the increasing heterogeneity of labour management practice and provide a strong contrast with the situation in the finance sector, where labour relations have been characteristically non-conflictual, where market conditions have differed from much of British manufacturing and where paternalistic values have imbued management thinking in several ways, notably towards the relationship with trade unions.

This book adopts the same sort of intensive case study approach for the reasons discussed above to elaborate the context of the labour relations strategies of the clearing banks over the last 20 years or so. It will demonstrate that the banks faced a highly complex set of business conditions and a range of constraints as well as advantages. Furthermore, the banks longstanding paternalistic values are argued to have contributed to the content and form of their labour policies. But as will be shown, these values have been refined as the business context has become increasingly competitive.

Oligopoly and Competition

As mentioned above, the banks developed their business in what is known as the retail financial sector, catering for private customers and corporate business. They provided, through their branches, a system of outlets linked to the clearing house which facilitated money transmission and debt settlement. The banks are essentially financial intermediaries. They make their money by taking deposits and lending on to other customers at a margin; to attract customers they traditionally did not levy a true cost for their services such as cheque-clearing, but subsidised these from the profits made by not paying interest on current accounts. At the heart of the banks' operational monopoly in the retail market was the ownership and control of the clearing system, and this contributed to the highly segmented financial market structure by placing a significant barrier to erstwhile competitors.

Within the retail sector the clearing banks did not traditionally try to provide for the same sort of financing need as the building societies, but they did compete with each other for deposits, that is, the savings of the personal sector (Boleat, 1980). The clearing banks traditionally lent on a short-term basis by the overdraft facility and also raised money by short-term desposits. Although their lending is often secured against assets of the borrower, it has been rare for them to take an equity in their customers' assets.

In contrast, building societies have customarily lent long term (for house purchases) against short-term deposits. Another major market — the capital market centred on the Stock Exchange — was also entirely distinct from the banking sector until recently, when banks started to acquire equity in stockbrokers and jobbers (see Rybczynski, 1984). For corporate customers the clearing banks also provided short-term funding, but there was little overlap between the functions of the clearers and other types of banks. The former were essentially deposit banks operating in the retail market, whilst merchant banks financed commerce and trade often through longer-term loans or an equity stake. A further effect of the monopoly position was that the degree of price and product competition between the clearers was minimal. This cartel was enforced by the explicit linkage between the banks' rate of interest and that charged by the Bank of England (bank rate) until 1971. Even after then though, the degree of price competition between the clearers has usually been minimal, in their view because the money markets are extremely competitive.

A further brake on competition after the Second World War was government intervention to secure its monetary policy goals. These affected credit and lending policies qualitatively and quantitatively. In particular, the slow growth of the banks in the 1950s was attibuted to the credit squeezes of that period (Nevin and Davis, 1970; Wadsworth, 1973) and thereafter these continued to be applied periodically in 'stop-go' policies. It prompted the clearers to begin their diversification policies in the late 1950s by buying into hire purchase and factoring companies to escape the most rigid application of these controls. This pattern of strong external regulation and limited competiton has been substantially disrupted over the last 15 years. Since the publication of 'Competition and Credit Control' by the Bank of England (1971), the official emphasis has been upon stimulating greater competition within the sector. One element of this new trend was the decision by the monetary authorities (the Treasury and the Bank of England) to make the banks declare their 'true' profits in 1970; more recently came the removal of the 'corset' on lending and the ending of exchange controls. The trend to greater competition has been continued in the *laissez-faire* policies of the Conservative government, leading to deregulation of the securities market, and the proposed liberalisation of controls on the building societies (BSA, 1983, 1984). But another factor in government policy has been consumer protection against possible business crashes or monopoly power (Rybczynski, 1984). This in turn has prompted continued influence over the internal affairs of the banks.

If the original pressure for greater competitiveness originated with the monetary authorities, the banks themselves welcomed it subsequently (Morse, 1981). One reason was that restrictions were seen to impede greater profitability and growth, especially because of their discriminatory nature (CLCB, 1978). Prior to 1970–1 the banks had competed principally through extension of their branch systems and expansion occurred very rapidly in the 1960s (see Table 2.1). A consequence of this rapid growth was that the number of staff employed by the clearers also grew substantially, despite the automation of the clearing systems then taking place. After the mergers of the late 1960s, however, rationalisation programmes began and numbers of branches fell by about 1,000 in the 1970s, although in some areas new ones were still being opened (National Westminster closed 750 and opened 350 in the ten years after its formation). Staff numbers did not fall as a consequence of this, however.

In the 1970s the central business strategy of the banks focused upon diversification. It was in this period that the overlapping of the discrete parts of the finance sector began as the banks 'became more growth oriented, more competitive and aggressive for new and diversified business, more profit conscious and less tied to traditional norms of behaviour' (Llewellyn, 1985, p. 24). Not the least important reason for

Table 2.1: Clearing Banks' Branch Numbers

Number:	10,886	11,804	12,315	11,838	11,659	11,289	10,993
Year:	1960	1964	1968	1972	1976	1980	1984

Source: CLCB Statistical Unit

this was the rising domestic inflation rate which tended to erode asset values (Morse, 1981). As a result, each of the clearers moved fully into international banking by acquisition, collaboration or the setting up of new businesses. However, domestically the volume of business also grew as the market for bank accounts was penetrated. The data in Table 2.2 demonstrate the long trend of growth in current accounts over the last 20 years. In 1976, 38 per cent of adults had a current account; by 1981, the figure was 50 per cent; by 1984, 65 per cent (IBRO). Similarly, the amount of account activity has continued to rise substantially, the volume of cheque clearings increasing by about 7 per cent per annum on average over the last 25 years (see Table 2.3), and this is projected to continue into the medium term (IBRO). Other financial activities were established or extended. These included insurance services; tax and trustee departments; merchant banking activities; credit card operations (Barclaycard was introduced in 1966 by Barclays Bank, Access in 1972 by the three other main clearers). National Westminster set up a computer-based payment transmission service (Centre-File) and the Midland acquired Thomas Cook, the travel agency, as well as a major marine reinsurance agency, Bland Payne (which it subsequently resold).

Table 2.2: Current and Deposit Accounts (000s)

	1972	1974	1976	1978	1980	1982	1984
Current accounts:	16,842	18,161	19,370	20,302	21,769	23,428	23,755
Deposit accounts:	9,402	11,012	11,378	10,929	12,227	13,143	18,299

Table 2.3: Clearing Activity, Volumes of Payments (millions)

	1960	1966	1972	1975	1980	1984
	753	1,084	1,557	1,953	2,860	3,551
Of which automated (non-paper transactions)	NA	NA	175	267	485	799

Market Environment

If the banks experienced growth and diversification in the post-war period, the market environment in which they operated became increasingly competitive. This can be seen by examining the trends in the markets for deposits and lending in which, until relatively recently, the banks basically identified only two types of customer: the personal account holder and the corporate one.

In terms of the personal market, Table 2.4 illustrates the growth and distribution over the last 25 years of the market for deposits. The banks' decline *vis-à-vis* the building societies was, in fact, a continuation of a pre-war trend as the housing market expanded but in the post-war period the decline meant they lost their pre-eminence in this market and now hold about 33 per cent. In contrast, the building societies doubled their market share between 1965–80, arguably because of the favourable tax arrangements for their depositors primarily (Vittas and Frazer, 1980) and by 1984 the building societies' total deposits were five times the size of the deposits gathered through the banks' branches. In reply, the banks and other financial institutions have had to offer more favourable rates on deposit accounts, putting pressure on their margins.

The main response of the clearing banks to this challenge was to

Table 2.4: The Deposits Markets

(A) 1963–79

	Banking sector % share	Building socs % share	National savings % share 54
1963	34.2	21.6	42.5
1972	34.5	37.8	26.2
1979	31.9	47.1	20.4

(a) Includes National Savings Bank, Department of National Savings and Trustee Savings Banks

(B) 1980–4 Market Growth in Value Terms (£m)

	Banking sector	Building socs	National savings
1980	6605	7715	1377
1981	3978	7082	4182
1982	3788	10294	3522
1983	3222	10250	2911
1984	3318	13249	3296

Sources: CSO Financial Statistics; Vittas and Frazer (1980)

expand their lending in the 1970s and extend the range of services offered. As the market grew in absolute terms, they held their share of advances but this did not resolve the deposit-taking problem. In terms of profitable margins, the banks gained much more in this period by the extension of their credit card businesses. These more than doubled their numbers of account holders between 1975 and 1985 and increased the value of their turnover (in money terms) by over four times between 1975 and 1980, and nearly three times between 1980 and 1985. In the 1980s the banks entered new markets such as that for house purchases, gaining 40 per cent of the market by 1982, although they subsequently withdrew somewhat to a share of around 15 to 20 per cent (*Bank of England Quarterly Review*, November 1984).

Strong competition also emerged in the corporate sector from the growing number of foreign banks attracted by London's currency markets. By 1970, total deposits of the American banks in London equalled those of the clearers and by the end of the decade, 20 per cent of lending to manufacturing industry was done by the US banks, half that of the clearers. Foreign banks (of which there are now nearly 400 in the UK) accounted for about a quarter of total corporate lending by 1984 (Davies and Davies, 1984). Although the volume of businesses rose dramatically in the 1970s, this competition led to a marked reduction in the margins on lending. Two key reasons appear to explain why these competitive trends were amplified from the end of the 1970s. One was the further liberalisation of the finance markets by the government (such as the ending of exchange controls and removal of the 'corset' on lending) which prompted the building societies and other retail banks, such as the Trustee Savings Banks, into greater competition.

The second spur to increased competition has been the accelerating pace of microprocessor-based technology. New developments in computerisation allow, for example, substantial competitive advantages in the securities markets through processing of higher volumes of business rapidly, and by giving instant access to information on prices in markets across the world. In turn, though, this allows other competitors to take advantage of the linkage of international markets. Advances in the automation of payments have also occurred; for example, the Clearing House Automated Payments System (CHAPS) went 'live' in 1984, allowing same-day payments for high-value items rather than the processing of paper such as cheques through the clearing system. These developments further facilitate competition from other financial institutions, as foreign banks, retail banks and the building societies also want to develop their markets.

Technical changes also remove the previously high barriers to entry to the banks' markets. Whereas previously a major network of branches was necessary to provide cash distribution facilities and deposit-taking, this can now be provided by automatic teller machines. Problems of scale economies and an adequate sized network have also been overcome by the sharing of facilities between several financial intermediaries such as building societies and other retail banks. In this way, new entrants hope to establish a niche in a market, drawing off some of the most profitable of the clearers' accounts without the costs involved in full-scale competition through a comprehensive branch system. In effect, then, the former strict market segments are breaking down and financial conglomerates emerging, raising the degree of competition in the banks' former monopoly preserve.

The operating environment facing the banks has thus been complex. Over the long run they have clearly lost their preeminent position in the personal sector and have had to contend with greater pressure from other banks as well as the building societies. Yet they have managed to sustain growth and profitability relatively consistently and to a much greater extent than manufacturing industry. Unlike the latter, the banks have not suffered decreases in demand through displacement in foreign markets and import substitution (Thirlwall, 1982). In absolute terms, their profits have been extremely large (Table 2.5). Indeed, as Morse has pointed out (1981), bank profits are to an extent counter-cyclical, rising in recessions as interest rates increase. This trend led to the windfall tax levied on the clearers in 1981. In reply, the banks argue that in recessions their profits do fall with increased bad debts, and that in real terms the returns on capital employed are insufficient and have been relatively stagnant (see the responses to Gryllis Report, 1981–2 in BIS, 1981b).

Banks also face the problem that because profits are significantly influenced by market rates of interest, they have little discretion over their margins. As Dunkley (1984) has argued, the banks' budgeting systems have been unable to develop a consistent pricing mechanism because of this external factor, and instead have allowed transmission costs to be subsidised by 'endowment' profits. Furthermore, the banks could not cope with prolonged periods of very low rates of interest, and Dunkley calculated that at the time of the Wilson Enquiry (1978), if the interest rate had fallen below 7 per cent, the banks would be incurring losses. Subsequently, the banks have argued that the breakeven point on current account business has risen (to 9 per cent in 1982) because of increased account activity and the decline in the real value of accounts (CLCB, 1981).

Table 2.5: Clearing Banks' Pre-tax Profits (£millions)

	Barclays		Lloyds		Midland		NatWest.	
	(a)	(b)	(a)	(b)	(a)	(b)	(a)	(b)
1972	106		75		73		127	
1974	141		127		94		120	
1976	198	279	145	206	167	244	188	265
1978	373	519	189	252	231	313	306	434
1980	523	413	305	244	230	125	415	331
1982	495	384	329	261	251	194	449	370
1984	655	548	468	406	135	56	671	576
1985	854	743	561	489	351	276	804	672

Notes: [a] Historical cost basis
[b] Current cost at 1985 sterling value.

This has had two effects. First, to intensify competition: hence the old agreement on mutually clearing the items of each others' customers without levying a charge on the customer has broken down and inter-bank charging has developed as the competition for accounts increases, although the banks are also being more discriminating in their attempts to extend their customer base. Secondly, the old system of cross subsidy in the account charging structure is breaking down as the banks attempt to analyse more precisely the costs and benefits of their services. At the same time competition means more costs have to be borne by the banks to retain custom. Yet meanwhile the profits from money transmission and current account balances have fallen as customers hold proportionately more of their funds on interest-bearing accounts. Together, these factors have forced the banks increasingly to pursue cost controls. This has inevitably involved labour costs.

In summary, then, the banks have operated in a market which has seen consistent growth in the post-war era. This has allowed them to extend their traditional business despite the intensifying competition from other financial institutions. But they have also pursued diversification strategies at home and abroad which, particularly in the 1970s, provided large proportions of their profits. In the 1980s, however, the technical innovations have thrown up the possibility that business expansion can proceed without rises in staffing, that competition from other institutions will continue to rise, and that the traditional patterns of employment will be disturbed as these changes take place.

Labour: Cost or Resource?

The long-term increase in business achieved by the banks involved a substantial increase in employment. Banking, like other service industries, has in the past been a labour-intensive industry with labour costs accounting for up to 70 per cent of total operating expenditure. Hence business expansion always involved a major rise in labour costs.

The labour intensiveness of the industry was in part a result of the banks' traditional mode of competition. As noted above, for many years the banks relied on expanding their branch systems as the means of gathering deposits and selling their products, and of extending business by gaining greater turnover on each service regardless of its profitability. Branches were given targets in terms of new accounts, lending and the marketing of various ancillary services, but the banks were growth rather than purely profit-oriented: indeed until recently they could not calculate or rank precisely the contribution of each account to profits. Each full branch traditionally also provided the whole range of services. It also kept its own accounts, balancing its books first manually, then on computer, on a daily basis. This required a substantial proportion of clerical labour tied up in the process of funds transmission and accounting procedures; in the mid-1970s, even after the installation of an 'on-line' network of terminals throughout their branches to perform the accounting, some 60 per cent of total staff were involved thus (CLCB, 1978). In other words, the majority of clerical staff have not been used as a means of marketing the banks' products nor directly for increasing business, but to process existing accounts. They have, accordingly, been regarded as an overhead rather than a resource to the banks. Until recently, it was only the most senior clerks or supervisory and management staff who actually sold the banks' products or undertook lending, and even today many may not have a formal marketing role in their job description.

The long period of employment growth in all of the banks provided a strong rationale for employer combination to minimise the risks of being bidded up in the labour market by the unions. Any bank that was forced to pay more than a competitor would experience a severe cost disadvantage. At the same time, because rates of profitability were to a certain extent unpredictable (being influenced by market interest rates) efforts had to be directed to containing unit labour costs by raising productivity. This was almost wholly associated with technical innovations to work processes. A key strategic objective of the banks was, therefore, to sustain a clear disjuncture between pay bargaining and productivity change, mainly by managing technical change at the enterprise level and pay determination nationally. For reasons discussed in Chapter 7, this strategy was also endorsed by the trade unions.

Managing the pay side of the labour cost problem has thus been closely associated with employer combination. For bargaining purposes the banks have operated together in the Federation of London Clearing Bank Employers since 1968, but this body is now undergoing substantial changes. One theme of the book concerns an examination of the conditions under which this employer body was set up, how it operated and why it declined in utility. In so doing, the following chapters look at how combination was reconciled with each bank's internal drive for increased productivity and the organisation of their labour forces at the enterprise level. A further associated issue is how national combination was reconciled with the pressure for greater enterprise control over pay. The issue of managing labour as a cost therefore also raises several questions about employer bargaining strategies in the contexts of changing product market conditions and of technological changes, and these are pursued in subsequent chapters.

Dealing with labour as the principle cost factor has thus been a central strand of the banks' operating strategies but, secondly, the banks have traditionally been regarded as 'paternalistic' employers, and have accepted this view of themselves (Blackburn, 1967; Sayers, 1957). In other words, they have encouraged an exceptional sense of identity between themselves as employers and their staff. Going well beyond a purely 'calculative' relationship (Etzioni, 1961), the banks have tried to create a strong normative commitment from all of their employees to their work and to the objectives of the organisation. Of course, white-collar employees have usually been thought to identify more closely with their employers' objectives than manuals (Strauss, 1954; Prandy *et al.*, 1983) but, in banking, the employers have sought to enhance this by a particular set of employment conditions and policies. Paternalism was thus to be seen as a strategy as well as a conditioning set of values.

In this case it appears to have been associated with the quasi-public function of the banks historically. The overtones of a public responsibility which went further than narrow commercial considerations meant that bank managers were to regard themselves as professionals with a responsibility to the community, able to dispense financial advice to their customers in a dispassionate manner and without necessarily trying to maximise the bank's financial interest. Significantly, one clearing bank until recently described the bank manager as a sort of financial GP, emphasising this 'professional' caring role in its recruitment literature. Furthermore, branch managers were not appraised soley in terms of financial performance, and were expected to establish social links with the local community to foster the good name of the bank in a manner which extended beyond the pursuit of new business.

Secondly, paternalism meant that the banks sought to 'look after' their staff. In particular, this meant that job security has always been a feature of banking employment and the 'hire and fire' image of brisker commercial environments was in some ways missing. As more than one manager pointed out, it was almost impossible to be dismissed from banking employment except for fraud. Additionally, the banks provided a range of benefits for staff, including subsidised loans for house purchase, generous sickness schemes and non-contributory pensions (Lloyds Bank has a contributory scheme). One manager put it thus: 'As a good employer, the bank wants to ensure that its staff have decent housing conditions, as well as working conditions'. In return, controls over the lives of their staff which extended beyond the employment contract were imposed; in the 1960s, for example, women were given a lump sum (a dowry) on marriage, on the assumption that they would be relinquishing their jobs, and some banks expected to be consulted about the marriage plans of any staff below a certain age. No management/staff division was perceived, and a highly unitary perspective of the employment relationship was prevalent (Fox, 1966). In particular, senior management has long believed that bank clerical staff identify with their own branch manager and are strongly influenced by his/her views on matters including trade union representation and the appropriateness of taking industrial action.

The identity of employer and employee has been also fostered by the reliance on internal promotion systems. This is a long-standing principle in all of the banks, dating from the last century (Sayers, 1957). Because in each bank most senior managers have all gone through the clerical promotion ladder, this is held up as evidence that the system is open and meritocratic, offering all staff the opportunity to advance providing they show ability. There is argued to be no stratification of rights or privileges, even if in practice there are wide differences in the prospects of males and females (see Chapter 6). Reinforcing this internal labour market is an informal agreement (again dating from the last century) between the banks not to recruit each other's staff. Hence, an employee's life chances are literally tied up with his own bank. A third aspect of the promotion system is that most staff have to acquire a generalist training, acquainting themselves with each clerical task in their careers. This system emphasises on-the-job training; hence experience does not necessarily enhance the external market prospects of the clerical staff, except in certain jobs such as cashiering. For the banks, this long period of clerical job experience provides a supply of labour for the high number of 'processing' jobs, and the ability to maintain a flexible workforce with a variety of enterprise-specific skills. As Marsden (1982) has argued, this is probably a necessary 'prop' if they are to offer lifetime employment regardless of product and labour market fluctuations.

Paternalism, fourthly, has influenced the banks' attitudes to collective representation. As it implies an exclusive focus of loyalty and reciprocal obligations from both parties, the employers traditionally resented external agents which challenged the authority of the employer. In practice, this meant the banks disapproved of trade union representation as incompatible with the 'professional' ethics of their staff. Trade unions were not seen as relevant to the employment relationship given the high identity of interests. Instead, the banks preferred to foster and deal with staff associations which embraced a more co-operative philosophy of mutual interests between staff and management, reflecting the paternalism of the employers. As will be shown, this co-operative philosophy has evolved quite considerably, not least because of the competitive pressures of the trade union which has sought to organise in this area. Nevertheless, the staff associations (albeit much reformed) remain well organised in banking.

In short, then, as well as the cost considerations, labour relations strategies were informed by paternalistic policies which set out to manage employees on the basis that they were a positive resource to the business. The objectives of this strategy were to maintain a level of commitment to organisational aims, to minimise the potential for conflicts of interest being perceived which could inhibit optimal performance of tasks, to generate motivation for the execution of relatively dull batch-processing jobs in the clerical area, and to insulate staff from the full effects of the external labour market.

This is not to suggest that paternalism necessarily conflicted with the objectives of controlling labour costs, nor detracted from the pursuit of profitability, for, like other paternalistic employers, the banks believed prosperity was entirely consistent with and the very basis of their role as 'good employers' (Child, 1969). Nevertheless, in the rest of the book the intention is to look at how paternalistic values have influenced management policies and have altered under pressure from the trade union and staff associations. Furthermore, the intention is to explore how labour strategies have reconciled the potentially conflicting demands of acting as fair employers with the growing urgency of unit cost control both within the bargaining system and without it. This, again, relates back to the influence of the growing competitive pressures in the product market.

Conclusions

In this chapter the link between the commercial context of the banking industry and labour relations policies has been examined. It has been argued that the banks have to be understood in terms of their market structure as an oligopoly with highly similar operational strategies and costs which resulted from the common reliance on the clearing system. The banks have faced increasing competition from other financial institutions and their shares of the total markets for deposits and advances have declined over the long term; on the other hand, they have shown sustained growth and profitability. Growth has in many ways been a labour-intensive process, however, and the need to recruit and retain large numbers of staff has been an important factor in the labour policies of the banks, particularly given the reliance on internal promotion systems.

In examining the labour policies, two distinct and occasionally contradictory factors were noted. The first conceived of labour as a cost; thus it was argued that efforts to control this factor were likely to underpin strategic thinking. Secondly, though, labour was perceived as being in a paternalistic relationship which extended beyond a simple 'cash nexus'. This, too, was likely to influence the development of policies, but potentially in contradication to the 'cost' influence, and this theme will be explored in subsequent chapters in relation to the nature, structure and limits of joint regulation; the substantive areas of the employment relationship, such as pay determination; and the relationships with trade unions and staff associations. Furthermore, the intention will be to explore how the intensifying product market competition and technological innovations have filtered through to the management of labour, given the substantial effects on employment levels, job prospects and career structures that these are having.

3 THE ORIGINS AND DEVELOPMENT OF INTER-UNION HOSTILITY IN THE BANKS

As a starting point, this chapter provides an historical account of the development of the institutions of employee relations in the banks. In so doing the intention is to emphasise certain themes which have been central to the strategic activities of each party. These include the importance of political influence upon the banks; the tradition of close co-operation amongst the employers, and similarities in their methods of managing labour; the traditional hostility to orthodox trade unionism which was subsequently tempered by the need for more formalised pay determination. The historical approach is also designed to give an insight into the relative absence of overt conflict, and yet to highlight the fact that discontent could emerge under certain conditions, which could in turn lead to institutional change. The chapter adopts a roughly chronological account of events from the formation of the first representative bodies and the modern clearing bank structure up to the formation of national machinery at the end of the 1960s.

The first forms of collective representation in the English clearing banks appeared around the end of the First World War, but it was only in the early 1950s that any sort of formal negotiating process developed. After a shaky start in which repeated attempts to form an industry-wide representative body failed, a permanent representative body emerged with the inauguration of the Bank Officers Guild (BOG) in 1917–18. Its membership grew quickly and by 1921 it claimed around 10,000 members, at that time representing about 35 per cent of the total bank staff. This coincided with a wider upsurge of interest in trade unionism among white-collar groups such as teachers and civil servants, but the growth of the BOG has also been explained by reference to certain structural features peculiar to banking (Allen and Williams, 1960). In particular, the growth in size of these enterprises through the increasing concentration of ownership was seen as important. By the end of the First World War a recognisable group of large clearers with national or near-national branch coverage dominated the industry after a rapid spate of mergers and take-overs, which stopped only with the intervention of the authorities (Colwyn Committee Report, 1918). As a result, bank work became more bureaucratic and greater central control led to formalised procedures and reduced the amount of local discretion. At the same time, rapid wartime inflation outstripped the rises in pay for bank workers and unionism appeared to be one response to the falling living standards.

Emerging in response to these general trends in banking employment, the BOG favoured industry-wide organisation. A further rationale for the trans-enterprise approach was also justified by virtue of the employers' policy of co-ordinating (informally) their pay structures and because the division of labour was similar throughout the banks. The Guild sought to recruit all clerical and managerial staff into its ranks (but at first not non-clerical staff such as messengers) and proposed industry-level discussion on the problems of bank staff. The idea of a national forum also appears to have been influenced by the Whitley system then being established in the civil service.

The BOG was not a militant body and deliberately distanced itself from manual unionism and the upsurge in strike activity in the post-war period. Yet shortly after its formation it was challenged by the creation of staff associations. These were certainly formed in some cases with management support and by 1921 existed in the five major clearers. Rejecting the BOG's objective of forming a single national union for all bank staff, the associations favoured domestic discussions. This domestic orientation was justified on the grounds that national trade unionism was inappropriate to the status of bank work and a national organisation was irrelevant given the domestic management of staffing matters and despite the informal employer co-ordination over pay. The associations did not request formal bargaining rights. Seeing themselves as a form of representation akin to other professional bodies, their objective was broadly to articulate the views of their members to senior management and vice versa rather than act as trade unions. At first relations between them and the union were not completely hostile and efforts to work jointly or even merge were made in certain banks, but these relations subsequently deteriorated when the banks refused to deal with the BOG. Evidently, employer policy strongly influenced the initial development of hostilities.

In the inter-war years formal negotiations over pay and conditions were not conceded to either body. The associations had informal consultative rights but were, in the view of Blackburn (1967), little more than passive management adjuncts. The BOG remained isolated, unable to enforce its recognition claims on the banks, and an intense rivalry with the associations began to develop. With the advent of war the picture changed somewhat: the BOG attempted to use Wartime Order 1305 to achieve its ambition of national machinery, and Barclays did grant limited rights in 1941, when the management of that bank believed (wrongly) that the union was about to succeed in obtaining a compulsory recognition order from the government (Tuke and Gillman, 1972). Much the same view was taken by the staff associations which therefore agreed to enter into discussions with the BOG with a view to forming a joint negotiating council for the industry, a proposition which was also supported by the banks on the assumption that if they were to be compelled to bargain collectively by the government it would be preferable to avoid dealing with the BOG alone. Mistakenly, the union took the view that it could achieve sole rights under Order 1305 and would not have to compromise its principles by co-operating with the associations. By stalling on the union's demand, however, the banks effectively bypassed the order and the BOG found it was unable to use the legislation to achieve sole rights, the Ministry of Labour being unwilling to enforce a recognition order upon the employers.

Despite this setback, in the post-war years the national union (which changed its name to the National Union of Bank Employees when the BOG merged with the Scottish Bankers' Association in 1946) continued to press for recognition. Instead, it was the staff associations which were recognised between 1952 and 1955 in most of the banks, ostensibly on the grounds that their membership was greater than the national union. There appear to have been two reasons for this move by the banks: first, to head off further statutory pressure to recognise NUBE; and secondly in response to growing staff discontent over post-war pay trends. The first factor related to the implementation of the Industrial Disputes Order (No. 1376) by the government in 1951, replacing Order 1305. This NUBE saw as a new opportunity to overcome the recalcitrance of the banks. As with the previous legislation, it allowed registered unions to invoke a national arbitration procedure in the event of an outstanding dispute: this included NUBE but excluded the associations. Making representations to the Ministry of Labour, the union demanded sole recognition but the banks pre-empted this by entering into identical negotiating agreements with their associations at domestic level, which effectively stalled NUBE's case.

But staff discontent was, also, arguably of importance to the banks in opting to introduce formal pay negotiations. It stemmed from the efforts of the banks to reduce labour costs by adjustments to the pay system after a period of over-recruitment before the war. This reduction had several dimensions. First there was an absolute decline in real terms of salaries of all staff compared to the pre-war period. By 1951 this trend was marked, as *The Banker* commented:

> But the fact remains that a clerk with 15 years service who did not receive any . . . special allowances in 1950 (except for a 17.5% or 20% cost of living payment) would have received at most 67% more than his predecessors did in 1938; this contrasts with a rise of 90% in the Oxford Institute of Statistics 'Salaried Cost of Living Index' between 1938–49, and a rise of 129% in average industrial earnings. It is impossible to give any comparable figures for changes in 'overscale' salaries (which are revised annually and which differ widely from bank to bank). (*The Banker*, November 1952)

Not only had real pay levels for most of the experienced bank staff declined, but in general, bank pay relative to the manual sector, where trade unions were operating and wages were more commonly regulated by collective bargaining, had also suffered. As Routh (1980) has shown, this decline in white-collar remuneration from 1938 onwards as compared to the manual sector was a general trend, but there is little doubt that it was a strong source of dissatisfaction for bank clerks, who regarded themselves as the 'aristocracy of clerks'.

Secondly, there was a compression of differentials. Between 1939 and 1951, there was a 100 per cent increase in the salary offered to clerks on entry into the banks at 17, whilst with 15 years' service, the increase in pay over the same period was 35 per cent (see Table 3.1). This trend of narrowing differentials was only interrupted in 1955. Thirdly, the banks' staff bodies were concerned about the practice of making non-consolidated bonus awards in substitution for changes in basic salary. This practice was adopted during the war, and continued until the late 1950s. The bonus, calculated as a percentage of gross pay, was usually unilaterally determined by the managements on the basis of changes in the cost of living but was not included in pension or sick pay calculations. In fact, the banks would allow these bonus payments to be repeatedly increased, rather than consolidated, over a period of several years, say from 1946 to 1953 for example, during which time the non-consolidated element had reached 27.5 per cent of basic pay. Furthermore, those staff over the clerical age-related pay scale (which ended at age 31 in most banks) were not guaranteed these bonuses, despite having to shoulder an increasing amount of work as business grew.

The reaction of the bank workers was not particularly militant. Most notably a petition on pay organised by NUBE in 1950 obtained the signatures of about 63 per cent of the 90,000 bank staff, far in excess of the union's membership of 30,000 at that time, and certain national newspapers ran sympathetic stories. It was, however, enough to alarm the banks and, in response, they insitituted formal bargaining procedures with their associations, backed by the provision of unilateral binding arbitration. This arrangement was instituted to overcome the problem that the associations were essentially powerless, being constitutionally and ideologically opposed to the use of bargaining sanctions. The difficulty this could present in the event of a disagreement had already arisen in the Midland Bank. Here, the association had been disbanded in 1950 after failing to agree over a proposed Christmas bonus, only to be reformed in 1953 with the Midland's chairman's blessing.

Table 3.1: Pay Scales, 1939–60 (indices in brackets)

			Women's Salary Scale			
Year		1939	1946	1952	1955	1960
Age	17	60(100)	135(225)	170+17(312)	220(367)	295(492)
	22	110(100)	210(191)	295+30(295)	350(318)	455(414)
	27	170(100)	270(159)	370+37(239)	450(265)	550(324)
	29			430+43(237)		
	31	200(100)	310(155)		505(253)	625(312)
			Men's Salary Scale			
Year		1939	1946	1952	1955	1960
Age	17	60(100)	135(225)	170+17(312)	225(375)	295(592)
	22	135(100)	210(156)	310+31(253)	350(259)	455(337)
	27	255(100)	355(139)	500+50(216)	600(235)	740(329)
	31	360(100)	480(133)	600+60(186)	700(194)	875(243)
Manager		900(100)			1,600(178)	

Note: Salary of a 'moderately successful', i.e. small branch manager.
Sources: *The Banker;* FLCBE

The arrangements also mirrored the provisions of Order 1376 for arbitration by an independent third party, and effectively excluded NUBE from any form of bargaining rights. It protested that the domestic agreements were a sham given the broad pay consensus in the industry, but in fact the institution of pay procedures with the associations does appear to have been associated with the ending of several elements of the unpopular pay policies throughout the industry. The practice of non-consolidatory bonuses was discontinued after the mid-1950s, the decline in real pay was halted and differentials stabilised, although not reopened.

Finding itself isolated, NUBE tried to reopen discussions with the staff associations on some form of joint working. Perhaps surprisingly these were taken up in 1954, possibly because of the interest shown by the Ministry of Labour which offered to act as an intermediary with the employers. Indeed, the associations and NUBE reached tentative agreement over the coverage and procedure for national machinery in December 1954, before the employers quashed the plan. Discussions between the staff bodies continued in 1955 on a spasmodic basis but were increasingly undermined by the resurgence of criticisms between the two staff bodies and finally collapsed at the end of the year. Henceforth NUBE had to fall back on its traditional strategy of trying to enforce a national negotiating forum via Order 1376, but this proved fruitless. It was left with the only option of trying to achieve a majority membership as the basis of a recognition claim, but aware of all the difficulties that this was known to entail facing hostile employers and strong competition from the staff associations.

1960–8: The Formation of National Machinery

Having established a system of domestic bargaining with the more co-operative staff associations, why did the banks opt for national machinery within a decade? The answer lies in a resurgence of staff dissatisfaction with conditions which emerged after 1960 and, when taken up by the staff associations led to a deterioration of their co-operative relationship with the banks; secondly, a degree of political pressure from the government and other external bodies was generated by NUBE's continuing attempts to have the staff associations outlawed. The importance of certain organisational changes in the banks and the key roles of individual senior managers in determining policy also has to be emphasised.

Changes in Pay Bargaining

From 1961 onwards, the associations invoked their arbitration rights in a series of references which over the following five years significantly disrupted the stability of pay determination in the banks. From the first reference, made by the Lloyds association, this action appeared to be justified, because the tribunal made a substantial improvement to the bank's final offer which it had attempted to impose unilaterally, after being rejected by the staff association. A Midland Bank arbitration then followed in early 1962, which again was favourable to the association and set the pattern for the rest of the banks. This was followed by the government pay controls, which the banks used as a justification for their pay offer, but which the associations interpreted as purely an interim measure. Hence in 1964, with the temporary ending of controls, the

Westminster Guild proceeded to arbitration and obtained a backdated increase for staff. Again, the banks felt they had no alternative but to follow the Westminster precedent, before incomes restraint was once again implemented.

Underlying these arbitrations was a growing division between the banks and the associations over the principles of pay determination. Particularly after the relaxation of official controls, the clearers began to expand their business more rapidly, and the decade of the 1960s was a period of substantial growth. Greater profitability resulted, as well as an increase in work loads, as new services such as the credit-clearing facility were introduced and the number of accounts and account activity grew. At the same time, employment levels were increased, but the staff associations began to claim that the greater demands on staff, particularly in senior clerical and supervisory jobs, were not adequately rewarded. In the 1950s the usual criterion adopted by both sides had been changes in the cost of living, but by the 1960s certain associations were basing claims on productivity both to justify larger general increases, and to enlarge differentials in favour of more senior staff who, it was argued, had shouldered the burden of growth in the banks' business.

Such claims were rejected by the banks mainly on the grounds that productivity was difficult to measure, and could not be directly related to the ability to pay. Their arguments were undermined, however, by the fact that productivity was increasingly being favoured by governments of both parties as the basis of pay determination (Barnes and Reid, 1980, pp. 30–40) and by the fact that banks did not publish their true profit figures. Evidently the arbitrators were more sympathetic to the associations' arguments rather than those of the employers.

There were, then, increasing difficulties for the banks with domestic negotiations. They were vulnerable to 'leapfrogging' claims to which they had to adhere if they were to retain comparable rates for their staff and they responded clumsily to the introduction of a new set of pay determinants by the associations by simply refusing to accept them as legitimate (Robinson, 1969). This lack of negotiating expertise was exposed as the associations won a number of the arbitration references. Organisationally, there were also innovations. In response to criticisms of dependence upon the banks, certain of the larger associations, and notably the Lloyds association, established greater financial autonomy, began employing their own officials rather than having them seconded and paid for by the banks, and applied to be officially registered as unions. An important contributory factor to the move to greater independence was the continuing criticisim from the rival body NUBE, which consistently criticised the associations as incompetent and the instruments of management rather than proper representative bodies.

The Cameron Report

Meanwhile the banks again came under pressure from NUBE after it made a further attempt to gain recognition by invoking outside assistance. Acknowledging that on its own it had little chance of enforcing change on the banks, NUBE turned once more to external aid in its campaign. Parliamentary representations were made in the late 1950s, and then the union filed a complaint to the ILO alleging unfair practices against four named banks.

The basis of NUBE's complaint made in 1962 was that these banks had attempted to promote workers' organisations (staff associations) which were under their control, thereby preventing NUBE from fulfilling its role as an independent trade union. Clearly, though, because the charge suggested that all the staff associations were employer-dependent, NUBE's complaint had general implications. It was, of course, denied by the banks both as being factually inaccurate and wrong in attributing the motive of control to their preference for dealing with associations. Instead, the banks argued that they had every right to select which union they wished to recognise. The ILO therefore proposed that the British government hold a fact-finding inquiry which would also 'endeavour to promote an agreed settlement on the basis of such an inquiry' (Cameron Report, para. 15). In response to this, Lord Cameron, a Scottish judge and industrial arbitrator of some experience, was invited to preside over the inquiry, and to report. His findings were published in November 1963.

Three points need to be noted about the report. First, on the specific allegations brought by NUBE, Cameron was in no doubt that the union's case could not be upheld. In the course of his highly legalistic proceedings numerous inaccuracies were exposed by the counsels representing the various banks and associations, and these in turn destroyed the weight of the underlying charge of domination by the banks. Secondly, Cameron refused to adopt anything but the narrowest interpretation of the role of the inquiry, so that NUBE's charge of a general strategy of domination levelled against the clearing banks was ruled outside his remit. Thirdly, however, Cameron did present some general remarks in his conclusions which were more favourable to the union. Cameron argued that the current arrangements were unsatisfactory, particularly to 'ordinary bank staff', many of whom, as NUBE members, were effectively disenfranchised. He therefore recommended NUBE be granted oral 'representative rights' in the four named banks. Furthermore, noting that there were a range of common features concerning all the banks, such as basic pay levels and recruitment of staff from the same labour markets, Cameron suggested this represented sufficient grounds for establishing a national negotiating forum, in which both NUBE and the staff associations should be involved. He emphasised, however, that it was not possible for him to compel the banks to do this — yet, less than a year later, changes broadly in line with those prescribed were proposed by the Committee of London Clearing Banks (CLCB).

It would appear, then, that the banks were strongly influenced by Cameron's proposals. Certainly in evidence to the Donovan Commission they implied as much (CLCB, 1965). Yet it is arguable that Cameron pushed the banks in a direction in which they were already going. The disutilities of domestic bargaining were increasing and a number of senior managers saw closer co-ordination through formal channels as the solution. Other factors reinforced this: one was organisational and stemmed from the growth in employment in the banks as they extended their branch networks in the context of tight labour markets; secondly, if NUBE was to achieve recognition in some form then employer co-operation was likely to be advantageous to meet the more aggressive union; thirdly, with a Labour government in power from 1964, it was thought that the banks would have to modify their hostility to trade unionism or face political pressure, perhaps via the TUC. Politically there were also other sound reasons for acquiescing to Cameron; in particular, the banks hoped to head off criticism over their accountability and specifically calls for the declaration of real profits, by compromising on the issue of representation. This is itself was an indication of the relative importance accorded to labour management by the banks' executives at that time.

Strike Action and the Establishment of National Machinery

However, opposition to NUBE's recognition, and thus national machinery, remained in two of the 'big five' banks, the Midland and National Provincial. Here the chairmen were both strongly opposed to trade unionism in banking and in such centralised organisations their views carried much weight in policy-making. Other managers were also not happy with the prospect, and when talks on the national constitutions commenced, the Midland and Coutts & Co. did not participate and National Provincial and Westminster (later merged into the National Westminster) were distinctly lukewarm; clearly, the combined size of these dissenting banks seriously threatened the viability of any future national machinery. Of the big five banks, only Lloyds and Barclays were in favour of reform and here again the chairmen's views were of importance in determining their policies. Furthermore, of the associations, the Midland was explicitly opposed to co-operation with NUBE, and the National Provincial also expressed reservations, though more concerning the utility of national as opposed to domestic bargaining. As for NUBE, its significant decision was to concede to Cameron's argument that it could not justify its claim for exclusive rights, thereby reversing its long-standing non-co-operation with the 'internalists'. Greater pragmatism became the dominant feature of its policy as recognition became its primary objective.

Notwithstanding these differences of opinion, by early 1967 agreement on draft constitutions had been reached. At this point, though, the talks collapsed with the withdrawal of the National Provincial and Westminster associations. Their respective banks then announced they could no longer participate and, with three of the big five absent the remainder of the banks also withdrew. At that point NUBE realised that ultimately it would have to rely on its own resources to achieve recognition. It proceeded quickly to adopt a new strategy designed to force recognition by the use of industrial action. But this was in fact the culmination of a less conciliatory approach by the union's executive, after the failures of the previous decade. Throughout the mid-1960s it was repeatedly argued at annual delegate meetings that the union could not expect employers to make concessions. Given the general opposition of bankers to joint regulation, they would only do so under pressure. This more militant approach was first tested outside the clearing banks, and appeared to pay dividends in a series of strikes in the TSB in the early 1960s through which NUBE obtained significant concessions and at the same time raised its membership markedly. A more forceful approach thus also seemed to be the means of resolving the union's long-standing problem that it was in the minority compared to the associations. If it differentiated its policies more clearly it would become a more attractive membership proposition.

Hence it embarked on a campaign for national machinery which it liked to two key issues, pay and hours of work. On both these issues it touched areas of wide staff discontent: the banks had been subject to tight pay controls after scrutiny by the Prices and Incomes Board since 1965 and pay rises had fallen significantly below the average change in earnings. Furthermore, the long-standing question of Saturday closure remained unresolved after several years of discussions among the banks. The difficulties were compounded when, after the end of Saturday opening was announced in 1966 in deference to staff feeling, the banks were subject to a Prices and Incomes Board investigation which opposed the idea as ill-conceived and against the interest of the public (NBPI no.106, 1967). The banks were thus torn between their role as employers and their function as a quasi-public service. Unsurprisingly, they refused calls from the associations and NUBE to negotiate on what they saw as a matter of business policy but they also declined to enter into any form of discussion, despite being aware of the increasing strength of feeling among staff. Heritage (1982) has linked this to the growing number of females employed in banking and routine clerical jobs. (In 1963, 59,080 (46 per cent) of clearing-bank employees were female; by 1968 the figure was 70,614 (51 per cent), but it was also arguably linked to the falling average age of the workforce. Certainly the banks argued that wastage was a serious problem, especially among younger females able to exploit a relatively strong labour market and without the career expectations or opportunities offered to male counterparts which might have tied them more firmly to the banks. Wastage among females was much higher than males, being 21 per cent compared to 8 per cent in 1967 and in the 18–23 age group the figures were 25 per cent and 15 per cent respectively (NBPI, 1967). Notwithstanding these problems, the banks acceded to the Prices and Incomes Board and also went further in proposing to defer Saturday closure, to extend opening hours and introduce an experimental scheme for late opening. Concern about competition for deposits apparently prompted the abrupt change of policy.

Evidently the banks had miscalculated the strength of staff discontent and this provided NUBE with the opportunity to develop a broad-based campaign which it called 'Action 67'. Through this it linked reform of conditions of work with the demand for national machinery. Mass meetings were held, branches were leafleted and the union tried to stimulate a broader discussion in the media. In terms of membership, the result was highly successful: during 1967 it raised its membership by over 30 per cent to 75,000 (see Table 3.2), the bulk of this rise coming between September and December.

Quite unprecedentedly, the union was also able to mobilise parts of its membership into strike action. A number of stoppages took place in late November and early December. Approximately 2,500–3,000 members were involved in each of the two days of action and although the union concentrated its action in its areas of highest density — South Wales and certain provincial towns in the Midlands and North of England (Nottingham and Doncaster, for example) — the branch-based pattern of union/associations membership meant that complete stoppages in any one area were rare. At most, the union knew that strike action could

Table 3.2: NUBE Membership, 1960–70

	Total	Clearing banks
1960	52,787	40,095
1961	56,458	43,191
1962	59,134	45,397
1963	61,458	46,417
1964	56,224	41,760
1965	58,444	43,721
1966	57,862	43,135
1967	75,513	58,778
1968	82,371	64,493
1969	87,043	67,849
1970	89,144	68,749

Source: Union records

have only a 'nuisance' effect on business but more significantly, it caused acute public embarrassment to the banks, as media comment was largely favourable to the union. The banks refused to re-enter discussions on national machinery, however.

NUBE therefore proposed to escalate the action by calling out a larger number of members throughout the country over the year-end period. As the banks audited their accounts then, this represented the first serious threat of disruption to their operations. More importantly it prompted the Minister of Labour, Ray Gunter, to intervene more forcefully. Until then the banks had discounted the matter as one of inter-union rivalry over which they were powerless to intercede and the minister had accepted this version of events. In previous meetings he had essentially aimed to avoid strike action by asking NUBE to rest its campaign pending the publication of the Donovan Report. However, the threat of escalating disruption led the minister to change tactics and press the banks to meet the union collectively. At the last minute the strike was called off (on 28 December) on the basis of this agreement to meet — the first the union had ever obtained from the banks acting collectively. At this meeting the majority of the banks agreed to restart talks on national machinery, and as of the big five only the Midland refused to participate, the proposition was a viable one. Subsequently, each of the associations followed the policy of its respective bank and only the Midland association stayed outside the talks.

Clearly, this change in employer policy was a result of a combination of the union's industrial action and the role of the Minister of Labour. Together these factors forced the CLCB to the negotiating table with NUBE to resolve the dispute over the heads of the recalcitrant associations. As a means of ensuring the associations joined the national machinery, the minister also proposed the resolution of the hours of work issue in the national forum. Given the deep divisions within the banks until then, and the existence of a small minority of executives ideologically opposed to recognising NUBE and determined to ride out its action, this intervention appears to have been a necessary precondition for change.

But there were also other pressures acting on the employers, including the fear of further investigations by the ILO; the possibility of the Donovan Commission proposing a statutory recognition procedure which might confer exclusive rights on NUBE; and wider concerns with government policy over central strategic issues including the disclosure of profits and hours of business. These left the banks particularly susceptible to government pressure at that time, whereas in the past they had been able to ignore it and indeed the Midland continued to do so.

Subsequently, facing the threat of further action by NUBE to force it in, the Midland's executives opted to join the national machinery as well; its association therefore reluctantly joined the staff side, and national negotiations on pay and the principal conditions of employment commenced in May 1968. Domestic rights were then offered to NUBE in joint staff sides with the associations in each of the banks in 1968–9 and by 1970 the union had secured its aim of bargaining rights for non-clerical as well as clerical staff throughout the clearers.

Conclusions

This chapter has discussed the historical development of institutional relationships and in the course of the narrative certain themes were stressed. First, this is an industry in which staff representation has always been divided between the national banking union and the company-based staff associations. The historical narrative highlighted how the rivalry between these bodies and their organisational and ideological differences were created and sustained by employer policies. Hence, the associations were started and encouraged by the banks as a means of avoiding recognition of the national union, which they saw as inappropriate to their industry. In many ways the BOG was, initially at least, as moderate as the associations; but many of its policies later became diametrically opposed to the 'internalists' whom it saw as part of a management strategy to obstruct trade unionism. The desire for national machinery and the belief that domestic negotiations were a sham exemplified this for although the banks' policy of co-ordinating pay levels provided a logic for national bargaining, it did not prove NUBE's long-held argument that national negotiations were intrinsically superior. Independent unions such as ASTMS, which subsequently entered the finance sector, have also preferred company bargaining but, for NUBE, the source of opposition to company bargaining essentially lay in its association with internalism. This rivalry was tempered by periods when inter-union co-operation was explored. Yet co-operation was essentially a strategy: a means to achieving recognition or extending bargaining rights in the face of employer obstruction. It was therefore always a fragile peace.

Secondly, this was an industry in which the staff bodies rarely demonstrated the organisational strength or the inclination to enforce their demands on their own. This was despite being highly organised in one body or the other compared to other white-collar workers in private industry, with an aggregate membership of around 70 per cent in the post-war period. Indeed, the associations explicitly disavowed the use of bargaining power through industrial action, and NUBE repeatedly based its recognition strategy on external support. The latter's fortunes and failures were thus related to the degree of compulsion the state would be prepared to exert over the banks to establish national collective bargaining. In the context of the voluntarist industrial relations tradition, this usually fell short of direct compulsion.

Changes in pay and working conditions were also clearly central to the development of the institutions of labour relations in the banks. The combination of a sustained decline in post-war pay relative to the inter-war years, coupled with a reduction in promotion prospects and compression of differentials, promoted the growth of collective organisation in the 1950s. Yet NUBE was unable to harness this effectively to obtain recognition, because it was pre-empted by the banks which introduced domestic machinery and offered some concessions in their pay policies. Furthermore, after 1958 the growth of the banks and the working through of the earlier over-recruitment began to improve the career prospects of male staff once more. However, another round of staff discontent over conditions of work presented NUBE with the opportunity to force home its recognition claim. In particular, the Saturday opening issue generated wider union support from the increasing number of female staff (Heritage, 1982). In so doing the national union showed a markedly more aggressive stance, arguing that bargaining strength rather than co-operation was now more appropriate.

In the employers strategies it is possible to discern a variety of often contradictory influences. The traditional ideological opposition to trade unionism was based on its incompatibility with the status of bank work. Unionism was also at odds with their paternalism, which was based on concepts of loyalty to the employer and identification with his objectives in return for security of employment for this implied there was no need for collective representation outside the firm. Yet such loyalty was clearly strained in the post-war period by thwarted career aspirations and declining relative pay levels. It also seemed less relevant to the growing proportion of female staff doing routine work. Efforts to constrain labour costs, particularly in periods of low growth, could thus conflict with the high normative consensus they expected from their staff.

Secondly, although opposed to bargaining with a trade union nationally, there were certain favourable functional aspects to industry-wide co-operation. These related to the banks' demand for labour and organisational growth. As they were recruiting the same sort of labour in a limited age range (15–18 yrs), they thought it necessary to minimise competition by maintaining similar salary ranges, particularly in the light of their rising need for staff in tight labour markets. Explicit co-ordination over pay via national machinery thus became increasingly attractive and was reinforced by the growing bargaining aggression of the domestic associations. The 1960s were therefore characterised by a dilemma between the ideological imperative of anti-unionism and the organisational imperative of co-ordinated negotiation. Ultimately it was resolved by the combination of political pressure (albeit indirect) and union opportunism.

4 MANAGEMENT STRATEGY: THE PRIMACY OF STABILITY IN THE 1970s

Introduction

In Chapter 2 it was argued that two somewhat contradictory factors have confronted the banks in their product market. On the one hand they faced growing competition for deposits from the personal sector, their traditional source of liquidity, and in the corporate sector confronted a growing number of foreign banks intent on exploiting the expanding Eurocurrency markets. Inter-bank competition was further encouraged by the authorities. In this environment the banks found margins were reduced. Indeed, further strain was put on them by the collapse of a number of banking companies in the secondary banking crisis of 1973–4 as the clearers had to fund a large part of the rescue package. None the less they have remained profitable: in part this was due to the international diversification strategies they pursued, but it was also assisted by the growing volumes of lending and the 'endowment' effect of higher interest rates at home. The banks continued to grow in terms of assets, employment and profits.

In this chapter the intention is to explore the consequences of these trends for the management of labour. It will be shown that the complex set of business factors fed through to a combination of policies in the area of labour management primarily designed to maintain stability. Efforts to improve efficiency were also made, but these were qualified in several important respects and remained of secondary importance to the need for continuity in the employment relationship and avoidance of conflict in the management of change.

How these changes were managed within and without the sphere of joint regulation and how the dual-level bargaining structure facilitated the management of stability and efficiency is also examined. To do this the rationale behind the broad scope of employer co-operation over pay-fixing is initially considered, as well as the strategies of the competing staff bodies with their opposing principles of ideology and organisation. Then the chapter looks at the major substantive labour relations reform, that of the pay structure, and the operation of the bargaining procedures with the arbitration facility. This is followed by a consideration of the non-negotiable areas of labour management in the enterprise to see how the objectives of efficiency and stability were carried through.

National Bargaining and Strategic Objectives

Choosing to co-operate formally in pay bargaining was in one important sense a move which went against the general tide of change elsewhere. Just as national bargaining was being established in the clearing banks, the Donovan Report (1968) was proposing institutional reforms to industrial relations which appeared directly to contradict the direction of change chosen by the banks. Donovan proposed the establishment of 'factory-wide' agreements in recognition that the 'formal system' of industry-wide arrangements could no longer be said to offer a satisfactory means of regulation. The banks had, however, never faced the emergence of what Donovan called the 'informal' system, located on the shopfloor, and, as several commentators have since pointed out, Donovan's analysis was heavily influenced by developments in the engineering sector (see Turner, 1968, for example). In particular, work-group negotiations over pay, facilitated by piece-work systems and with extensive shop steward representations, had not developed in the banks. Pay remained highly centralised and there was no evidence of earnings 'drift' except through overtime payments necessary to cope with increased business volumes; following the introduction of computerised accounting, the amount of overtime worked appeared to fall (Winton, 1982). There was no evidence that job controls were an obstacle to management prerogatives, and certainly neither the national union nor the associations challenged managerial rights to organise work as was seen fit for the needs of the business.

Formalisation to regain control of the shopfloor and earnings 'drift' did not, therefore, lie at the heart of the banks' reforms. Rather, national negotiations provided a means of co-ordinating pay and minimising the chances of experiencing 'leapfrogging' (Deaton and Beaumont, 1980). This was important as banking was labour intensive and at this time the banks were expanding their branch systems. The result was that between 1965 and 1970 the numbers employed by the London clearers rose 22 per cent to 176,875 (CLCB, 1978). High demand for new and replacement staff in identical labour markets provided the logic for formal co-ordination of pay levels and synchronisation of pay changes.

Nevertheless, the scope of national co-ordination was exceptionally broad. It included all clerical staff between the ages of 16 and 31 (i.e. those on the age-related pay scale) who, constituted about 80 per cent of total staff and also fixed the minimum managerial and minimum retirement pay points, thus influencing the pay levels of those groups of staff not included in national machinery, the senior clerical, supervisory and management staff. In doing this, the banks therefore opted to establish common or very similar pay rates for career and non-career clerical staff, leaving little room for manoeuvre at the company level.

Some banks had proposed a smaller two-tier model which would establish minima nationally for junior staff, creating a clearer distinction between the levels of determination of pay for career and non-career workers. After all, the banks were only competing for staff at the point of entry; above that their internal labour markets functioned rigidly, reinforced by 'no-poaching' arrangements for each other's staff so that theoretically each could pay what it wished for more senior staff. Against this the banks had to bear in mind that, at least for the increasingly large number of non-career (mainly female) staff, differences in pay rates at any clerical scale point might affect recruitment. Moreover, the entry rate set a floor for the whole scale; changes in this rate would reverberate through the scale with significant cost effects. The external labour market could therefore still have an effect well above the ports of entry to the internal market, particularly in the conditions of high demand for clerical staff in the wider economy.

The coverage of national machinery — its 'comprehensive' scope — thus related to the banks' similar demand patterns for labour which was in turn determined by their oligopoly in the product market. But forming an industry-level body did not entail a complete delegation of control over pay determination. The federation was a forum which, because of its small size, allowed each bank to take an active part and have a strong input into decision-making. Furthermore, as the prevailing method of determining pay was then by age, there was no great cost in forgoing the domestic discretion. This might not have been the case had the banks sought to link pay either to enterprise performance or to some measure of individual effort. Such a rigid pay-for-age system might have appeared to contradict the highly developed internal promotion systems, but it reflected the traditionalist values then predominating which emphasised experience or seniority rather than merit as the basis of career advancement. In turn, this related to the emphasis upon stability and caution in a business environment of relatively limited competitiveness.

It was in this sort of situation that the paternalistic notions of loyalty and security had been able to thrive. They were explicit in the banks' attempts to introduce a no-strike agreement during the negotiation of any item through the procedure, but NUBE's executive would not accept this. The union did agree to the banks' proposal to a unilateral arbitration facility which effectively minimised the likelihood of industrial action, however.

By creating a national forum, the banks concomitantly established certain important protections for their prerogative. Although operating above the enterprise level involved some loss of managerial control, it offered the advantages of distinguishing between negotiable and non-negotiable issues more clearly (Sisson, 1983) and of divorcing the process of bargaining from the point at which management policy was set (Kinnie, 1982). This was illustrated in discussions prior to the setting up of the national machinery when the staff bodies proposed to make pensions negotiable and to make automation and conditions of work open to consultation. Resisting these suggestions strongly, the employers argued they were matters of domestic concern and thus beyond negotiation. Secondly, drawing a clear line between pay and non-pay items meant joint regulation was confined to the market for labour in determining the main norms of the employment contract; it did not mean the staff bodies were to participate in what have been called the managerial areas of regulation, governing the utilisation of labour and other factors of production (Flanders, 1975). This was because rules determined in the national arena had then to be applied in the enterprise in a quite separate process where individual business conditions had to be taken into account but in questions of implementation the unions were excluded.

Thus the bargaining model did not conform to the dynamic type in which rule-making and rule-application were part of the same process (Clegg, 1979). For example, overtime rates were fixed in the national council but it was up to managers in the branches to determine the level of overtime to be worked in their office and how it was allocated. At the heart of this distinction was the structural division between national joint regulation and enterprise management, yet this was not undermined by the subsequent introduction of company-level bargaining because these agreements were deliberately designed to operate independently of the national pay forum. They were not concerned with interpreting nationally agreed rules and only covered matters that were not negotiated nationally. Unlike other models of multi-level bargaining, the second tier did not modify the industry scales in the light of local conditions: national rates were actual conditions of employment. Significantly, the company agreements also excluded any negotiation of any issues of labour utilisation, although they did permit consultation, unlike the national agreement. This facility was designed to allow a looser management of change by agreement without impeding managerial prerogative.

National machinery also represented a means of containing the inter-union rivalry. For even while NUBE had remained unrecognised it could consistently criticise the staff associations as ineffective, thereby potentially undermining the negotiated agreements: NUBE's 1967 campaign on pay and hours had apparently been very successful in this respect. There is also evidence to suggest that in response to competitive pressure the associations became more 'unionate' (Blackburn and Prandy, 1965) and thus less amenable to management objectives. It is notable, for instance, that in the 1960s several associations began to organise themselves more independently from the banks after the publicised criticisms of NUBE to the ILO, and it was those most opposed to co-operation with NUBE which became most aggressive in domestic negotiations and pressed claims to arbitration before having to come into the national machinery. Whilst this sort of competitive pressure did continue in the joint machinery, the joint staff side at least meant that this competition did not spill over into the bargaining process.

Stability and Efficiency: Pay Reform

Having looked at the implications for the parties of the adoption of a system of collective bargaining at two levels, the remainder of the chapter explores how the banks' desire for stability worked through this system. But it also illustrates how the banks cautiously began to pursue efficiency-based changes.

The major issue which stimulated this latter objective is the reform of the pay structure initiated at the beginning of the 1970s. The background to this was the Labour government's incomes policies which tightly constrained the banks for nearly five years between 1965–70. The problem facing them was the Prices and Incomes Board's close scrutiny of the banks settlements. The board increasingly saw productivity as the key determinant of pay rises, but this implied a focus upon the enterprise as the best level at which productivity changes could be measured and instigated (Fels, 1972; Liddle and McCarthy, 1972). As this threatened to disrupt the co-ordinated pay structure, it was resisted by the banks. Only when a revised set of proposals from the board in 1969 (NBPI no. 106) offered the opportunity of a compromise by recommending an industry-wide productivity reform to link pay to task rather than to age did the banks acquiesce to the idea of change. This is not to suggest they were uninterested in efficiency gains, but the prime means of achieving these was seen to be coming through technological innovations such as the computerisation of branch accounting and clearing automation. Hence, to start bargaining over productivity would also effectively mean having to *buy* staff agreement to new technology.

It was, then, under the initiative of the NBPI that the banks actually began to plan efficiency-based reforms. They were, however, aware that the existing system was proving inadequate. Labour turnover was rising, especially among female staff. They constituted over 50 per cent of employees by 1970 but were not expected to reach managerial rank and were more susceptible to external market conditions. Winton (1982) quotes turnover figures of up to 30 per cent per annum for some areas (notably London) in the junior female grades. Growing discontent also emerged over the increasing substitution of younger female labour to perform previously more senior tasks such as cashiering. This led to substantial variations in the pay of people doing similar tasks and working alongside each other.

The reform package was, therefore, a compromise which sought to satisfy a number of differing objectives among the parties. One of the central objectives was to develop a task-related pay structure more accurately reflecting the external market pressures which would help the banks recruit and retain staff. It would also satisfy the Board's objective of increasing efficiency through a more meritocratic pay system, while if a national job-evaluation system were used, the co-ordination on recruitment rates and basic-grade salaries could be maintained. Such a reform was also acceptable in principle to the staff bodies which had been pressing for changes. In particular NUBE had already proposed a task system before its recognition (NUBE, 1965) through which it hoped both to overcome the constraints of the pay policy and also provide more for the growing number of non-career staff. Similarly, the associations supported reform as a means of resolving staff dissatisfaction and generating greater efficiency for the banks. Predictably, the main area of contention between the staff side concerned the level at which the reform strategy was formulated rather than the concept and assumptions of restructuring itself. The associations argued that it was a domestic issue and wanted to use the opportunity for the reform to reduce the area of national negotiating; NUBE, being still unrecognised domestically in some clearers, insisted it was a matter for national negotiation. The matter was resolved by the banks, a majority of whom remained committed to the existing scope of national bargaining and supported the NUBE position.

Negotiations over the proposals lasted throughout 1970 and under the new system a task-related pay structure assessed on a points rating method of job evaluation was introduced for all clerical staff. Four clerical grades were created nationally, with one bench-mark job for each grade. For example, the cashier job was fixed as the bench-mark grade 2 job throughout the banks. However, additional domestic grades could be established by any bank (Barclays has two extra clerical grades, National Westminster has none), and apart from the bench-mark jobs any other clerical tasks could be allocated according to domestic level discretion. This was because, firstly, although the points-rating system of job evaluation was developed nationally, its application was interpreted domestically. Secondly, because job design remained a matter for managerial control at the enterprise level, the content of similarly named jobs (foreign clerk, safe custody clerk) could vary between the banks.

This reform was significant in several ways. Its strength lay in the way it preserved a sufficiently common framework for the national machinery to continue, with a comprehensive 'scope' covering all clerical grades and thus grouping together career and non-career staff, but at the same time offered a degree of domestic autonomy and did not impinge on the enterprise-based control of work organisation and labour utilisation. Secondly, it reconciled a number of competing aims. Although the banks had not originated the reform, they subsequently embraced it because the trend to greater competitiveness in the product market was beginning to filter through, prompting the need for policies which emphasised achievement rather than seniority. Formerly, the system of rewards by age had reflected a set of values which stressed work experience rather than actual task performance and placed a premium on loyalty. By removing the barrier of age as the qualification for progression, the new system was designed to enable those staff who demonstrated merit to move more rapidly up the organisation.

At the same time a task-based pay structure represented a solution to the strong pressure from the external market. It provided the means to retain large numbers of experienced clerical staff even if they were not designated for managerial careers. They, too, were offered career progression (albeit less extended) and with that a more flexible pay progression in order to solve the problem of excessive turnover. So on one level the reform was designed to reduce the inequities of the old age-based system but, on another, the new pay structure provided the basis for a more systematic segmentation of the labour force. It served to formalise and accentuate on already existing dual labour force structure based broadly on sex; but it must be noted that the dualism was not based on differences in conditions of employment between primary and secondary segments. Ostensibly, employment opportunities for all entrants were equalised and the revised pay structure ended the difference in male and female pay rates, by introducing a single clerical rate. Rather, the extent and rate of career progression became the basis of differentiation within the labour force.

The Management of Inter-union Competition

The second area where the objective of stability was paramount concerned the management of the tension between the union and associations and here the strategies of the banks also shifted. Initially the paternalistic policies implied a limited area of joint regulation and continuing support of the associations in preference to NUBE. This was subsequently modified to a more accomodating approach to both sides, particularly in the two banks where external personnel experts were brought in; in the others a more ambiguous attitude to managing inter-union competition remained.

For NUBE the agreement to co-operate with the associations represented a victory for its more pragmatist wing which saw recognition as the prime objective for the union. In opposition to this strategy there was always an undercurrent of criticism from the more purist members who regarded co-operation with the associations as a betrayal of the union's principles, and who had dominated in the past at key junctures. Yet this difference was purely one of means for the common objective of the union was sole bargaining rights through the demise of the associations. Co-operation was thus a means to this end. In part, of course, this co-operation was the result of an acknowledgement that NUBE could not on its own enforce its claim for exclusive recognition. Yet there was considerable optimism that NUBE would quickly achieve this aim despite its compromise. In late 1967 the union's executive was arguing it was 'within an ace' of the majority membership which would give it control of the staff side, believing that the rapid and exceptional growth in membership during the latter half of 1967 would continue. Although the union entered the joint staff side as the minority body, it was confident that the support for the associations would wither as the union demonstrated a superior performance as a bargaining agent.

Clearly there were several assumptions in this train of thought which subsequently proved to be questionable. One of these revolved around the motivation to join a trade union. Other things being equal, it was assumed that potential members would prefer NUBE because it claimed to be more effective through its more aggressive bargaining posture. Hence, the prime reason NUBE had remained the minority staff body in the banks was because it had never been able to demonstrate this superiority by competing on equal terms with the associations. The evidence partially bore this out as well: in the one bank where NUBE had similar rights to the domestic association — Barclays — it had established a majority position. In short, NUBE assumed a highly instrumental motivation which largely discounted organisational factors or issues of 'character' in determining the choice of union.

The union believed it could demonstrate this superior effectiveness in the process of bargaining in the joint staff side. But because it had traditionally condemned domestic negotiations as a sham, the union was prepared to accept initially that it would be limited to national recognition. Subsequently, it reversed this and pressed for domestic bargaining rights but still portrayed these as of secondary importance, because they seemed to legitimise the internalists' case. In so doing, the NUBE voluntarily limited its range of bargaining to those matters which were common to all banks. By definition, therefore, it did not envisage trying to extend the area of joint control beyond pay and conditions despite the emphasis upon demonstrating a superior effectiveness. The historical experience of discrimination thus fundamentally conditioned the union's objectives in a way which concurred with the employers' objectives in establishing national machinery. Yet the possibility that the limitations of joint working, the reliance on conflict resolution through arbitration and the neglect of local organisation and negotiation might represent a contradiction with the strategy of demonstrating a greater effectiveness did not apparently worry the union, such was the optimism created by its successes in 1967.

For the associations, national machinery evidently entailed a fundamental compromise with the internalist doctrine of an enterprise-based relationship. Yet their flexible response indicated their basic pragmatism. Their internalist ideology was not a constraint because it had never been an elaborate and fixed body of principles but a loose descriptive term derived from and subordinate to practical action. Internalism stressed co-operation and saw the domestic bargaining relationship as appropriate to occupations such as banking given the high job security, the opportunity for career advancement within the firm and the high trust, paternalistic management policies. Yet it had not in the past precluded discussions with NUBE or examining the prospect of national machinery, except for a 'hard-core' minority, if institutional survival was seriously threatened.

This flexibility was central to the ability of the associations to survive competition from NUBE. In the post-war period it meant that they were transformed from passive, dependent organisations and according to Robinson (1969) cultivated greater sophistication in their bargaining strategies. In terms of their internal organisation and function as bargaining agents, it is possible to accept Blackburn's (1967) argument that they became more 'unionate'; but they remained distinctive from other 'orthodox' white-collar unions in some ways and particularly in their opposition to the use of industrial action or identification with the rest of the union movement through affiliation to the TUC. One factor which was crucial to the retention of a distinctive co-operative ethos was the availability of unilateral arbitration. It provided them with a source of power which obviated the need for sanctions and meant they could claim to be as powerful as NUBE yet sustain the relevance of their co-operative ethos. Nevertheless, the lesson of 1967 for the associations was that they had to remain sufficiently responsive to changes in the employment relationship and the potential for white-collar militancy which required a more robust approach. In turn this depended on certain external factors and notably the sorts of strategies the banks were to deploy, as well as the policies and performances of the national union. And here the subsequent stability in many areas of the employment relationship, despite the rapid technical changes and reform of the pay system, were crucial to the associations' ability to evolve without crisis.

The division of representation thus offered certain advantages to the banks as long as it could be contained in the bargaining process. Although the continuing moderating influence of the associations was thought crucial, the banks did begin to sponsor rudimentary lay structures for NUBE in the early 1970s. Full-time seconded representatives were introduced between 1971 and 1973 to deal with individual grievances, and the union gradually gained other facilities such as the use of banks' internal mailing systems and noticeboards. At the same time, the banks continued to support the internalist bodies indirectly by allowing them to rent offices at discounted rates and paying the pension contributions of those officials seconded to work for, and formally employed by, the associations.

It is also apparent that although the banks favoured a merger between the staff bodies they were ambivalent about this in practice. The two formal rounds of merger talks that took place in the 1970s are discussed in detail in Chapter 7, but here it is worth noting the views of the banks. On the one hand the division was considered to be a natural expression of employee interests and beyond the responsibility of the employers; on the other hand, they had long assumed an interest in the structure of representation and recognition. Hence the banks were never prepared to impose 'order' by forcing a merger and indeed arguably sustained it in so far as they continued to provide organisational support for the associations and BIFU to operate independently. In discussions in the Employers' Federation, the proposition that the banks could use sanctions or the enticements of broader rights to end the division was always rejected; concern was also expressed over the character of any merged body, the priority being to sustain the associations' influence. In short, the employers' desire for a more efficient bargaining structure was always moderated by the traditional paternalist preferences.

This is demonstrated by considering the more interventionist approach adopted by the two banks where personnel specialists were appointed from outside the industry. In Williams and Glyn's the merger between NUBE and the staff association was achieved largely through management pressure. Here the union was in an exceptionally strong position, with a majority of members, while the association lacked the resources and size of the others. Nevertheless, the division of representation continued under management blessing until a personnel director was appointed from outside the banks. He stressed the need for bargaining efficiency with a stable 'mainstream' union and overturned the previous policy guaranteeing recognition to the association. On the recommendation of the Commission on Industrial Relations, which was called in to investigate the position, the new merged body was given extended rights to appoint lay officials at branch level and a participative structure at all levels in the organisation was established with the union (CIR, 1973). Employees were encouraged by the bank to join the union, although an agency shop was not granted. This sort of relationship was a considerable departure from the norm in the other banks, and much more in line with the orthodoxy then prevalent among personnel specialists (Batstone, 1984; Thomason, 1984).

Similarly, the Midland Bank's policy on union relations was influenced by the drafting of personnel specialists into the organisation from outside. The bank had historically had an unusually close relationship with its association and correspondingly had been very hostile to the union. Indeed this caused the internal body problems in so far as its financial reliance on the bank meant it could not develop the sort of resources needed to expand its membership and only met the criteria laid down by the Industrial Relations Act for registering as an independent union with difficulty. It was pushed into a merger with ASTMS in 1974, preferring that union to NUBE, it would seem, mainly because of the personal animosity between various officials. The bank thus found its paternalistic policy had backfired: it faced a strong TUC union which also opposed national bargaining on principle, and was forced to suspend all existing procedures. This meant that with NUBE only having 27 per cent of the staff in membership, a large majority were not represented for pay purposes by any body.

The key management changes took place in 1974–5 with the appointment of Sir (later Lord) William Armstrong as chairman and in the personnel department the appointment of a new general manager and assistant general manager from outside the bank, the latter coming from the CIR. The instability of the industrial relations arrangements was declared by the chairman to be a management priority and the personnel department was able to develop, with his support, proposals which sought to restore stability by extending union facilities as the sweetener for joint working. The proposition was received with some hostility by senior bankers who favoured minimal concessions and even considered the re-encouragement of a staff association but, with the endorsement of the chairman, it was undertaken. In practice, formal joint working between NUBE and ASTMS floundered as competition between the two in other areas of the finance sector increased (Willman and Morris, 1985). None the less, a measure of informal joint working was established in job evaluation and health and safety committees, for example, before separate but identical procedures were signed at the end of 1978.

In the other banks where the personnel function was headed by bankers rather than career personnel experts the prevailing paternalist ethos ensured some doubts about domestic-level initiatives to encourage a unified representative body. Here the associations were all stronger organisationally and had higher memberships than NUBE (see Figure 7.2). Yet even where merger discussions were explored between the union and an individual association, as in Lloyds in the mid-1970s, the bank did not opt to encourage this. Indeed, there was some concern expressed in the Employers' Federation over the initiative as, with the extra members NUBE would take control of the staff side. Stability was thus seen in terms of containing the influence of the orthodox trade union and continuing to support the associations.

Arbitration

The banks' original concern for stability is also evident in the bargaining procedure they adopted. Yet here again pressures to achieve greater control over the costs of labour subsequently emerged. The procedural device adopted nationally and at company level to ensure stability was a unilateral arbitration facility. Unilateral arbitration was first introduced into the banks' negotiating arrangements in the early 1950s. Then, it had reconciled the non-coercive philosophy of the staff associations with the appearance of meaningful negotiation, for either party could refer a difference to an arbitration panel when the procedure was exhausted and each was bound by its outcome; hence the unilateral nature of the facility.

In Chapter 3 it was shown that references to arbitration only occurred after 1960 but quickly became frequent. The banks were unhappy with this but, in instituting the national machinery, it was thought crucial to retain the facility for several reasons. First, the inter-union conflict was seen as potentially destablising to the bargaining process even with a joint staff side. Secondly, it would preserve the staff associations' non-coercive policies and obviate the need for them or NUBE to deploy sanctions. Thirdly, NUBE was feared as an increasingly militant union and if it subsequently gained control of the staff side it was thought vital to have arbitration to avoid disruption. For its part, to ensure that its position was equal to that of the associations, NUBE was keen to have an arbitration facility in the procedure, the long-standing experience of hostility and discrimination once more influencing its judgement. History also suggested that its members were by and large of a moderate disposition and likely only to back a call for action in exceptional circumstances. Arbitration was therefore a safer option than free bargaining.

At national and company level the procedures were extremely tight. Usually only two failures to agree were allowed before bargaining was exhausted and the matter was then referred to a tribunal; no conciliation clauses were introduced and it was inferred that failures to agree would be registered in any matter that had not been resolved at a single meeting of the negotiating council. Little room was left for negotiation to develop fully, yet between 1968 and the end of 1977 only nine references were made nationally and sixteen domestically (excluding Technical and Services staff (T & S) negotiations). Johnston (1978) argued that this demonstrated the good faith of the parties at the bargaining table and certainly there is evidence that a number of devices were developed informally by the negotiating council to offset the rigidity of the procedure and avoid being drawn into a reference before bargaining was really exhausted. These included an extended phase of discussions prior to formal negotiating, particularly on pay; the suspension of the procedure and shift to a discussion phase in the middle of the negotiations which was often minuted, and the use of side-meetings which were usually off the record.

Further evidence that arbitration did not undermine collective bargaining, as some have argued it might (cf. McCarthy and Ellis, 1973), is suggested by the skewed distribution of the references. Nationally, three arbitrations took place in the first eighteen months whilst between 1973 and the end of 1977 only four occurred, of which one was a clarification of an earlier tribunal. Domestically the references were more evenly spread with nine in the first half of the period of joint working and seven in the second.

To an extent experience taught the parties how to work round the tight procedure. Yet the uneven distribution was not so much due to bargaining immaturity as the intractable nature of the issues first facing the council at the national level and certain starting-up difficulties. In particular, there was a backlog of complex outstanding matters. Notable among these was the question of Saturday working, an issue which was further complicated by disagreement over whether it was strictly negotiable: the banks claimed that opening times were a matter of business prerogative but this was rejected by the staff side which saw the issue as one of working hours, and thus negotiable. For tactical reasons, therefore, the staff side was keen to see this arbitrated to establish its negotiability permanently. The other complicating factor at the outset was the differences between the banks in the standards of the items not previously negotiated. Much time was thus spent in trying to standardise principles, as for example with regard to the focal point and boundaries for the coverage of the London allowance, and in the absence of prior norms the procedure was quickly exhausted.

Nationally and domestically the arbitrations were nearly always called for by the unions. At the company level the motive was almost always to establish or reinforce the principle of comparability between the banks, whilst each bank would essentially be trying to maximise its own area of discretion, by establishing substantive differentiations on the basis either of managerial custom and practice, or arguing that operating standards were not analogous. An example of this occurred in an arbitration in Williams and Glyn's Bank in 1977 when NUBE made a claim for revised management salaries to bring the scale into line with National Westminster. The bank rejected this argument on the grounds that job evaluation systems differed and thus the managers' job varied between the banks. In this case it appears the bank was vindicated in so far as the award made no explicit affirmation of the principle of comparability when setting out the revised scale. A second basis of comparison was the national agreements: if a holiday increase was gained nationally, for example, and then not passed on to those staff covered be the domestic agreements, this would invariably be contested. Overall, the greater frequency of domestic arbitrations can be explained by these twin comparability pressures upon each bank.

Although most references to arbitration were made by the staff side it can be argued that neither side gained or 'won' more than the other. Wherever possible, the tribunals tried to develop equitable solutions by splitting the difference between the claim and offer, although where conflicting bargaining principles were involved this was not possible. Only in one national arbitration not explicitly hinging on conflicting principles was there an unequivocal victory for one side, i.e. its final bargaining position completely matched the details of the award. This effort to reach a compromise was reinforced by the composition of the tribunals which would consist of a side-man or wing-man nominated by each side to put their respective cases plus the independent chairman. Most chairmen would endeavour to reach a unanimous decision and as the evidence of previous bargaining process was submitted to the tribunal it became effectively an extension of the negotiations rather than an entirely distinct form of rule-making (cf. Johnston, 1975). As Kahn-Freund has noted, the distinction between voluntary bargaining and compulsory arbitration could be more fluid in practice than it is conceptually (1977).

However, the banks did become concerned about the operation of the arbitration facility and considered its modification or replacement. Informal proposals to extend the procedure or insert a conciliation stage were made more than once but rejected by the staff side. The banks' dissatisfaction centred not so much on the actual costs of the awards, or because arbitration extended the range of joint regulation, but because of the restrictions arbitration placed on the *future negotiability* of various items — its 'trapping' effect. This occurred because quite simply no award lapsed or was superceded without the joint agreement of the bargaining parties, nor was any time limit placed on the operability of an award by any tribunal. A decision once reached could thus stand regardless of changed external circumstances.

Secondly, the trapping effect occurred when an award established the principles governing future negotiation if the reasoning behind the decision was detailed and explicit. For example, the large town allowance, paid to staff working in towns above a certain population size, was explicitly correlated with the London allowance in a reference in 1972, although no such formula was proposed by either side. Thereafter the two allowances were automatically adjusted together, having previously been negotiated independently. But even when tribunal decisions were not so explicit, the parameters of future bargaining could be set by comments on the sorts of factors deemed to be relevant or irrelevant which the arbitration panel made in giving the award.

Arbitration also restricted the possibility of switching bargaining levels, thus further limiting flexibility. Once an item was confirmed as arbitral, and this effectively occurred if both sides agreed to negotiate on it, then it remained arbitral at that level only. This frustrated the banks several times, most frequently on the vexed question of late opening which each bank was keen to extend in the early 1970s to counterbalance the effects of Saturday closing. Because patterns of demand varied between the banks they pressed for domestic discretion, but ran up against consistent opposition from the staff side which refused to let the matter be taken outside the national machinery.

This tendency to 'trap' or limit the parameters of future bargaining was at the heart of the employers' dissatisfaction with compulsory arbitration. To an extent it related to the managerial criticisms commonly raised against third-party rule-making: that decisions are taken out of the hands of those responsible for the running of the enterprise, and that arbitrators have no expert knowledge of the enterprise and usually lack the facts to make the soundest judgement (Institute of Directors, 1984). Furthermore, the 'trapping' effect had cost implications, both direct and indirect for even though there was only one arbitration on national pay awards, this did not mean that arbitration was not taken into account in the bargaining process. As Dufty (1978) also found in his case study, the parties were affected by assumptions of what might happen in the event of a reference and this influenced their negotiating positions. Bargaining occurred within a context of potential arbitration and to avoid this the banks were usually prepared to settle generously. In effect, they valued the flexibility of free bargaining even if there was a premium attached.

So, something of an ambiguity in employer priorities emerged in the 1970s. Although the long-standing method of dispute resolution, arbitration, was increasingly perceived to have disadvantages as the question of controlling costs and the prerogative to manage labour efficiently came to the fore, it was thought to have secured the objective of avoiding outright conflict, to have preserved the power of the non-coercive staff associations and to have sustained the image of the banks as fair employers in the eyes of their staff. It was thus assumed to be a significant contributor to stability in employee relations and no move away from the existing systems was thought justified.

Enterprise Level Management

Partly this was because at the enterprise level, where the focus was primarily on the effort side of the employment relationship, the banks enjoyed unilateral control. As with the national level policies, the overriding approach was one of caution and the growing commercial pressures thus only fed through in a qualified way. Nevertheless, some refinements of the controls on labour utilisation in each of the banks did occur.

First, the management of work organisation became more systematic. The organisation and methods (O & M) functions were expanded, especially under the stimulus of two factors, the on-line computerisation of the branches and the application of the job evaluation schemes for clerical and then managerial staff. In the mid to late 1970s the O & M departments were integrated into the management services function in each of the banks and these were upgraded to be headed by a general manager. Under the auspices of these O & M teams, clerical work measurement was started in the mid-1970s to assess labour requirements more precisely. From actual and expected volumes of accounts and lending demand, the central O & M function began to determine manning levels and distribution of clerical and supervisory grades more precisely than in the past. In this way the corporate control of productivity levels became tighter. However, this was not associated with a major revision of standards and there was an underlying continuity in the methods of work and the allocation of clerical tasks.

Secondly, formalised systems of employee assessment were introduced. Standardised appraisal procedures implemented after the job evaluation exercise established more uniform measures of factors such as quality and speed of work, replacing the old system which had been based much more on subjective assessments from branch or departmental managers. This implied a more objective basis of performance measurement, strengthening centralised control over career paths. But meritocratic performance involved more than the demonstration of technical skills. Strong emphasis was placed upon a range of attitudinal factors — to work, to colleagues, appearance — which were as much designed to shape the desired organisational persona and engender commitment to the employer as to establish technical efficiency.

Associated with this more explicit structuring of the labour force was an extension of formal training. This was used to develop technical skills and thus to augment the 'on-the-job' learning which was the traditional method and meant that all recruits had to gain experience of each clerical task before they could progress. Those within the higher tiered groups were systematically exposed to a wider range of tasks through frequent transfers across the whole range of group activities. They also received broader training in lending and risk assessment and in the 1970s the banks each extended their in-house training facilities for managers, Barclays opening a residential group management training centre in 1975, for example.

Thirdly, the qualified pursuit of efficiency was also apparent in the management of pay. Domestic-level pay negotiation was re-introduced with the salary reform of the early 1970s specifically so that the banks could use pay as a motivator. Domestic scales were established for each grade over and above the national scales to reward exceptional performances. In practice, however, the commitment to performance-related pay remained heavily diluted. At best it could constitute a premium of around 5 per cent in a year for the most competent performance, and the modal payment was between 2–3 per cent of basic pay. Secondly, staff had to work through the national scales in each grade before they could reach the domestic scales, a process taking several years in most cases. Thirdly, the banks restricted the size of increases in the domestic scale to those agreed nationally to avoid too much grade overlap and fourthly, once the performance-related payment was made, it was consolidated into the basic salary. Collectively, these factors meant that rather than being designed to act as a performance motivator in the short term, it was more of a cumulative premium which only became significant in terms of a long period of employment. It encouraged solid loyalty rather than exceptional performance. Long-term career progression thus remained at the heart of the banks' motivation strategies and their use of pay to generate greater motivation was highly circumscribed.

At the enterprise level, therefore, even without the constraints of joint regulation, change was cautious and limited. Standardisation and centralisation of control occurred, but these trends were not associated with radical adjustments to the required levels of effort. Accordingly there was relatively little variation in the systems or standards of each bank.

The reasons for this picture of limited change can be understood by remembering that the banks were not unsuccessful commercially in this period. Growth in numbers of accounts, payment transactions and lending occurred at an unprecedented rate. The domestic divisions proved consistently profitable despite the development of stronger competition in several areas of business. In addition, international diversification and the credit card subsidiaries generated substantial funds for the clearers so that the aim of labour management was essentially to sustain a stable operating environment. Moreover, the banks had found a way of containing their unit labour costs whilst they grew which obviated the need for stricter control over their staff or dramatic reforms to generate greater intensity of effort. This solution was to automate more of the processes involved in branch banking and the clearing system and through this to generate the productivity increases necessary to grow profitably, as will be shown in Chapter 6.

Conclusions

In their labour relations strategies the banks were predominantly concerned to maintain stability during the 1970s. An avowedly more profit-conscious management ethic and stronger competitive pressures made little impact upon the management of labour except to stress the value of conflict avoidance. Extreme caution followed the introduction of national wage negotiations and recognition of the union, NUBE. Stability was strongly bound up with constraining the union's influence both over the range of items open to negotiation and by harnessing it to the associations. The use of arbitration at the national and company levels also reflected the value of conflict avoidance to the banks.

Potentially, one source of strain upon this stability was the reform of the internal labour market. In placing greater emphasis upon meritocratic systems of promotion and reward the banks sought greater efficiency by creating a clearer distinction between career and non-career staff. Yet many elements of continuity offset the impact on the staff of this: greater productivity did not require major attempts to intensify effort levels or work loads. Standardisation of work methods and levels did not lead to dramatic changes in work effort. Most importantly, because of the product market growth, job security and career progression could still be offered and through these the traditional high-trust relationship could be sustained. Hence the success of labour management was built on continuity in job content and satisfying the expectation of career/salary progression; co-ordination of pay to minimise the risk of instability in managing tight labour markets; and underlying this, continuous organisational growth. A final factor aiding this was the willingness of the unions to endorse the direction of change and accept the broad limits on their power.

5 REVISED OBJECTIVES: EFFICIENCY AND COST CONTROL IN EMPLOYEE RELATIONS

To recapitulate, the prime change the banks have faced is one of increasing competition and market interpenetration as the barriers between various parts of the finance sector have broken down. Underlying this have been two factors, technological innovations and liberalising or deregulation policies pursued by the government. The changes caused by these factors mean new forms of money transmission, deposit-taking and lending can be developed without extensive and labour-intensive branch systems, providing competitors with the potential for significant cost advantages. In marketing terms a clearer segmentation of customer groups has replaced the general growth policies of the 1970s. These trends are not simply the result of a more mature product market but reflect a more intensively commercial approach in the face of increased competition. The consequences of this for employee relations are explored firstly by looking at the changes in the institutional relationships between the banks and the staff bodies nationally and at the enterprise level in this chapter. Then in the next, the implications of technological change, which is central to new modes of competition, are examined.

Arbitration

In the last chapter it was shown that the unilateral arbitration facility operating at the company and national level was valued for several reasons. Despite some concern over its trapping effects among the banks, after the collapse of the joint staff side in 1978, the banks were in favour of reintroducing similar procedures because they minimised the risks of industrial action, buttressed the co-operative philosophies of the staff associations and banks and enhanced the idea of a fair employer with interests similar to those of its staff. Indeed, because of the open antagonism between the unions, a discussion document circulated in the Federation of London Clearing Banks Employers in late 1979 concluded that arbitration was even more important to avoid competitive bargaining. One alternative proposed was to recognise only one union, but it was thought injudicious to choose BIFU (for ideological reasons and because it was the minority union) or for the staff unions alone (as they were not represented in the Midland and Williams and Glyn's and this could provoke BIFU into a rerun of its successful 1967 recognition campaign). The situation remained in limbo from 1978 to 1980 while merger talks between the unions took place, but when they collapsed greater instability developed and pushed the banks into a decision.

At the same time the banks wanted to continue to co-ordinate pay despite the non-functioning of the national forum. This proved to be difficult in the context of the ending of the pay policy in 1979 as it was followed by a period of high wage settlements. The banks were subject to two years of extended leapfrogging in negotiations which were conducted domestically (in 1979 and 1980), failing to co-ordinate objectives or tactics and conceding to competing claims and threats of action. BIFU used its strategically powerful data-processing members as a vanguard in these campaigns with little cost to itself. The difficulty of dealing with competing unions suggested that a formal procedure which guaranteed conflict resolution would be valued. The solution favoured by the Federation and the majority of personnel managers was to work towards reopening arbitration arrangements to secure bargaining stability, but no solution could be established which ensured that a tribunal involving one union would be binding upon the other.

Meanwhile, a different set of priorities had begun to emerge among the most senior executives of the banks. These emphasised the urgency of cost control as bad debts rose in the recession and criticism of the banks' profitability at home through the endowment effect of high interest rates grew, resulting in the special tax on bank profits in 1981. This coincided with growing instability in bargaining at the company level, where arbitration agreements remained intact. These bargaining units became the focus of a series of references as each side tried to use the arbitration facility to demonstrate its power. In Lloyds the staff union, which had sole rights for management grades, took a claim to a tribunal in 1980 over holiday differentials. For its part, BIFU made a sequence of claims in Williams and Glyn's where it had sole recognition. It then attempted to undermine the national pay agreement made in 1981 between the banks and the CBU through a domestic claim. In this context the suitability of arbitration was re-examined.

This coincided with certain reforms in the government's approach to its own industrial relations. Expressing its support for greater reliance on market factors in pay determination, it disbanded the Comparability Commission and subsequently endorsed the Megaw Report proposal to end unilateral arbitration. This change of policy had a pronounced influence upon senior managers' thinking in the banks and combined with the internal problems facing them, was sufficient to end the attempts to resume unilateral arbitration in the banks. Instead, the model adopted by the Midland Bank in the late 1970s was taken up more widely in order to introduce greater flexibility into the management of employee relations. However, in the Midland the problem was slightly different as BIFU confronted ASTMS rather than a staff association, but the latter had never had national negotiating rights. ASTMS was also the minority body in membership terms. The Midland's solution had been separate but identical procedures, each incorporating a conciliation stage bringing all the parties together and it was the option of conciliation that was taken up by the other banks, although no joint union co-operation could be achieved. This minimised the risks of conflict while not curtailing the bargaining process.

The dangers of this strategy were recognised, though. As the Federation director argued at the time, without arbitration the associations would be exposed as powerless and this could have important consequences for the representative organisations. Either the associations would be forced to become more militant in order to be effective, in which case the banks would lose any advantage of the co-operative approach, or BIFU might attract greater support. Furthermore, defenders of the old procedure argued that in 'splitting the difference' management had not been penalised significantly, particularly as arbitration was seen as an important component of the banks' image as 'fair employers', sharing common interests with their staff. Ultimately, though, pressure from senior general management prevailed, over-ruling the more stability-oriented policies of the personnel specialists.

One expected consequence of the move away from arbitration was an increase in industrial action, but since 1982 the number of disputes has remained low. For BIFU's part it is arguable that the reason it has not undertaken more action is primarily that it cannot galvanise its members to do so. Except in 1983 it has balloted them for action over the pay round every year and in 1983 it actually held a national strike (its first in the banks for 16 years). This was over the extension of Christmas opening, which was done in response to competitive pressures, but the action was only partially supported and appeared to make little impact on the banks, thereby revealing BIFU's weakness in the existing division of representation.

More success has been achieved with certain types of local action, principally over technology-related changes either for redundancies or new working patterns. This is particularly the case in the Midland, where

BIFU's density is higher than average, it does not face a staff association, and the job losses have been comparatively severe. Local action forced managers to reopen decisions on the changing shift patterns at the Heathrow Airport branch in 1984 and in the northwest over branch restructuring. None the less, in other banks where BIFU is in the minority to a staff association, it has also claimed local successes — in Lloyds' Jersey branch over work reorganisation and in National Westminster over redundancy plans for messenger staff displaced by new automated payment systems (CHAPS II) in the City of London. In other respects BIFU's success with local action and its 'vanguard' strategy of using its powerful data processing staff members to lead its action has been curtailed by the banks' separation of computer and engineering staff into other bargaining units.

Another cost of abandoning unilateral arbitration was the corrosion of the co-operative policies of the staff associations. As the banks predicted, this threatened to expose the associations as powerless and to force them to revise their policies to become more unionate. Yet while each has threatened to press for industrial action, they have also been reluctant to dispense with the co-operative ethos. Partly this is because bank staff still appear unwilling to endorse militant policies and the fact that BIFU has not achieved significant gains by militancy has relieved the pressure on the staff unions to demonstrate greater effectiveness by the use of sanctions. Partly it reflects the associations' need to remain distinctive in image from BIFU as the basis of their competitive advantage. Nevertheless, the banks have had to cope with increasingly frequent threats of action from both unions and this has destabilised the bargaining relationships.

Pay Determination

Complementing the shift in policy on arbitration has been a changed approach to pay determination and again a more direct influence over the negotiating process by senior executives. To understand this shift it is necessary to look at the position in the 1970s when the Federation was dealing with the joint staff side.

In this period, market forces strongly influenced the bargaining policies of the banks. Table 5.1, showing the rise in employment between 1970 and 1980, indicates the strong demand for labour throughout by the banks which meant in effect that they could be trying to recruit up to 30,000 entrants in one year. Most of these would be school-leavers starting at the most junior grade. The entry-point salary thus acted as the base point from which the pay levels of the rest of the grades were set. At the same time clerical employment was expanding in the rest of the finance sector and the public sector, so that the banks felt themselves to be pay 'followers' in a generally tight market. Comparability with external rates became the standard or base determinant for settlement projections, if only to avoid staffing shortages and excessive turnover.

Table 5.1: UK Employment in the London Clearers, 1970–80

1970	174,033
1974	197,448
1978	207,341
1980	231,451

Source: FLCBE

Yet other factors were also germane to their strategies. Repeatedly in Federation meetings there were references to the need to sustain staff morale by 'reasonable', i.e. not minimal, agreements; that it was necessary to take a longer-term view on pay rather than just maximise short-term benefits; and in the context of the income policies implemented by both Labour and Conservative governments that although there were good reasons for supporting these it was important to 'do the right thing by their staff' in order to retain loyalty and commitment.

Such statements may have been prompted partly by the uncertainty and distortions created by official controls but, as higher inflation persisted, the banks clearly loosened their pay principles. Initially, no linkage was accepted between the rate of inflation and pay levels, then this was taken as the basis of pay determination; by the end of the decade the banks had moved to building in an allowance for future inflation.

Closely linking pay either to enterprise performance or to commercial prosperity was avoided, however. Although profit-sharing schemes were introduced in the mid-1970s partly to enhance motivation and commitment, these were not linked at all to basic pay levels. The problem in establishing an enterprise-based calculus of salary levels was that it would generate inter-firm differences; thus in 1978, when a measure of productivity bargaining was allowed under the Social Contract, the banks effectively ensured that the productivity premium was standardised. More fundamentally, the strategy of avoiding a productivity-pay linkage was necessary if the banks were to be able to remain profitable with sharply rising business volumes. The principles of pay determination thus comprised a mixture of factors including market considerations and concerns with fairness and morale and implied that bargaining should incorporate a degree of flexibility without being linked to corporate performance. Flexibility was further encouraged by the threat of an arbitration reference which might fix disadvantageous pay principles. The banks were in effect prepared to pay a premium for the privilege of free bargaining, with the result that rises in real pay were readily acceded in the 1970s.

But having re-established their co-ordinated position over pay bargaining in 1981, the banks then adopted a deliberately tougher line. A series of lower settlements followed. Although this coincided with general trends in the economy, Table 5.2 shows that the banks' settlements in the period 1980–5 were below the rise in the Retail Price Index. One explanation for this may lie in relative union weakness. Not only do the unions lack the support of the arbitration facility, but since 1982 their division has been exploited by the banks which have secured a settlement with one union and then implemented it over the head of the other. Clearly such a policy has high risks, particularly when the settling union is the CBU as in 1983 and 1985, as this left the Midland and Williams and Glyn's to implement a settlement without agreement with the body (or bodies) representing their staff, but it is further evidence of the determined stand the banks have adopted.

Table 5.2: London Clearing Banks: Salaries Relative to RPI, 1972-85

	CGI Minimum	CGI Age 21	CG2 Age 21	CG3 Minimum	CG4 Minimum	Minimum Managerial
1 October 1972	100	100	100	100	100	100
1 January 1973	104.7	104.7	104.7	104.7	104.7	101.8
1 January 1974	117.7	107.7	106.2	104.4	102.6	101.8
1 August 1974 (including threshold consolidation)	132.9	121.9	120.3	119.5	117.9	112.4
1 July 1975	130.4	119.7	118.4	117.1	115.2	110.2
1 July 1976	142.4	126.9	120.7	117.4	113.0	102.9
1 July 1977	131.4	115.4	108.7	104.5	100.7	90.8
1 July 1978	141.7	116.2	109.2	106.1	102.1	94.6
1 July 1979	149.8	122.5	115.4	113.0	108.7	101.6
1 April 1980	153.8	126.0	119.1	117.4	114.3	108.4
1 April 1981	150.4	123.2	116.4	114.6	111.6	106.1
1 April 1982	147.9	121.0	114.4	112.7	109.7	104.1
1 April 1983	148.5	121.5	114.9	113.1	110.0	104.5
1 April 1984	148.5	121.5	114.9	113.1	110.0	104.5
1 April 1985	149.1	122.0	115.4	113.5	110.5	104.9

Note: An arbitration adjusted salaries in the London Clearing Banks from 1 October 1972.
Source: FLCBE

The banks' uncompromising approach is also evident in their bargaining behaviour. Rather than enter an extended process of negotiation in which compromise between offer and demand gradually narrows the difference, they have consistently been unwilling to move far from any opening offer. Since 1982 these have usually been backed by pamphlets justifying the offer, distributed to staff in an attempt to seize the propaganda initiative from the unions and thus to weaken any efforts to mobilise their members for action. Managers have also been requested to put the employers' case to their staff in branches and offices. Coinciding with this more uncompromising position has been a reluctance to entertain conciliation at ACAS, although this has taken place at the behest of the unions. Requests for arbitration to settle claims by the unions have been consistently turned down.

Competitive pressures have also fed through to the pay criteria favoured by the employers. Replacing the previous preoccupation with comparability in the labour market is a more pronounced concern with the ability to pay. Slacker labour markets may help to explain the shift, coupled with the relative fall in demand for staff illustrated in Table 5.3, but none the less, the banks are still recruiting substantial numbers of young people. But the new bargaining criteria also arguably reflect an ideological shift, being designed to reinforce the identity of the employee with the organisation, by seeing his/her fortunes as intimately linked with those of the bank rather than the broader industry trends. Hence the argument goes that profitability, which is crucial to future expansion and the best guarantee of employment, requires cost/wage constraint as real profit levels are inadequate. Short-term employee benefits must be tempered in the interests of longer-term organisational prosperity.

Table 5.3: UK Employment in the London Clearing Banks, 1981-5

1981	223,237
1982	227,594
1983	229,553
1984	229,241
1985	231,846

Source: CLCB

Linked to these changes is the greater influence of senior general management over the process of pay determination. This arises from the view of corporate management that all costs must be constrained more effectively and, on the grounds that labour is such a major cost item, pay determination has inevitably been affected. The example of Barclays illustrates the size of potential savings where 'Every percentage point on our costs means £10 million for the UK division' (quote by deputy general manager in Turner, 1985), but these internal objectives also coincide with external political pressures.

To an extent the banks have traditionally been subject to close scrutiny by government. As large employers they were thought to have a significant impact on settlement trends in the 1960s and 1970s and the centralised pay system also rendered official control relatively easy. Yet even in the free bargaining environment of the 1980s, the process of pay formulation has been subject to certain external influences similar to the sort of political contingency experienced by public sector trading monopolies (Batstone *et al.*, 1984). The banks' chairmen have usually received strong signals to limit settlements close to those budgeted for the public sector and the RPI with the tacit possibility of sanctions (such as extra taxes on bank profits) representing a major incentive to co-operation. This means the process of fixing bargaining parameters has changed in such a way as to reduce the role of personnel managers in initiating pay proposals; instead they are now confined to implementing decisions and clarifying the tactical aspects of the bargaining process.

As commercial performance has become a more important determinant of pay for the employers, the logic of enterprise bargaining has appeared more compelling. Increasing organisational diversity arising from the application of technical innovations has also reduced the utility of the common national framework. This culminated in the Midland and Williams and Glyn's leaving the Employers Federation in 1985. In the Midland's case one important reason for leaving the Federation was its relatively low profits in the first half of the 1980s and in Williams and Glyn's the merger with the Royal Bank of Scotland to form a UK bank meant membership of the London Federation was inappropriate. In both cases the option of domestic bargaining was also enhanced by the difficulties presented by divided unionism, and the fact that neither recognised the CBU.

Apart from this, the scope of national agreement has generally been loosened as individual banks have taken initiatives over issues which have become stuck at the national level, such as reform of the pay scales in the junior grades and the proposed removal of the large town allowance paid to staff working in certain provincial towns. So, although the Federation has in some respects been able to transmit changing enterprise considerations relatively rapidly into the bargaining agenda, it has not stopped a general trend to a new enterprise-level focus. The reform of the banks' relatively indulgent pay strategies suggests the rising competition in the product market has taken the role of the national forum past its peak.

Enterprise-level Relationships

As a counterpart to the changes at national level which centred on controlling wage costs and restricting the influence of the unions, domestic policies have been mainly directed towards the maintenance of stability in the period of turbulence in the product markets and in inter-union relations.

First, there has been a more explicit effort to manage communications with staff. This reflects a paradox in that, as the business environment becomes more competitive the need for staff co-operation and commitment increases, yet uncertainty is more likely as the old assumptions about job security and career progression are eroded. Communicating the need for change thus becomes more important. It has involved new methods of direct communication and the better co-ordination of existing mechanisms such as bank newspapers and circulars. Management thus now give more thought to the purpose and content of their communications mechanisms and have devoted extra resources to this.

Associated with this is a renewed interest in monitoring attitudes and conveying to staff the competitive context behind corporate strategies. For example, Lloyds' senior general managers undertook a series of meetings with their branch managers around the country using a video presentation to show the bank's business plans in 1985. The banks have also explored ways of tapping into 'shopfloor' expertise to improve efficiency along the lines of Quality Circles being used elsewhere, although the highly standardised operational systems and the lack of a physical product are thought to make Quality Circles themselves inappropriate. Lloyds has perhaps gone furthest along this road with a network of work-groups being set up in its head offices to examine the scope for efficiencies and savings, called an Activity Value Audit. It plans to extend this scheme in a modified form to its branches in due course, having guaranteed that no compulsory redundancies would result from any proposals. National Westminster introduced staff meetings in the mid-1970s as a form of industrial democracy and have recently begun monitoring these centrally as well as using them as a means of communicating the bank's policies. Barclays has also instigated a series of consultative committees at local and head office level as part of a policy of greater employee involvement. Through these committees senior management intend to communicate the need for and direction of change and, by obtaining staff views, to anticipate the likely problems in the adjustment process. In effect, there is a general trend towards actively seeking to reinforce the understanding and commitment of staff to business objectives. Such direct communications policies are similar to innovations elsewhere in British industry (Batstone, 1984).

Yet secondly, this has not led to a reduction in union consultation, but is rather a parallel development. Consultation has arguably been extended over the past five years into areas such as the introduction of new technology, staffing levels and appraisals. The latter issues have always been regarded as strictly within the managerial prerogative but, without arbitration, consultation can shade more easily into negotiation and in this sense the area of joint regulation has never been wider. The introduction of staff annual meetings at which staff representatives directly selected from the branches as well as union officials are invited to hear presentations from senior managers and question them on policy also indicates the parallel nature of this development of consultation channels. Behind this is the intention to maintain direct contact with staff rather than allow the unions to monopolise the flow of information, as is perceived to have happened in manufacturing industry and contributed to lower levels of trust.

Thirdly, the union's lay structures have been extended. This started as a managerial initiative in the early 1970s when representatives from each union were seconded from the banks to process grievances but not to negotiate on collective conditions. Subsequently the number of seconded representatives was increased, but more recently restrictions have been placed on the number and role of the seconded representatives by two of the banks and more generally they have consistently resisted any tendency for these lay officials to negotiate manning or job standards. Additionally, the Midland and Williams and Glyn's, the two banks which pursued the most accommodative union relationships, introduced office representative schemes at local level in 1978–9 decentralising grievance representation and incorporating health and safety duties. By 1985, only Barclays had not followed this policy. As Willman and Winch (1985) found, albeit in the very different environment of the car industry, it appears that managers here are keen to promote union representation insofar as it may facilitate the settlement of individual problems through union representatives but are opposed to any extension of joint regulation which might impinge on the terms of the effort bargain.

The fourth factor which illustrates the attention to stability concerns the scope of domestic bargaining. In particular, the banks have opted to keep their growing number of computer services staff in a separate bargaining unit at the enterprise level. In isolating them the banks have attempted to minimise the potential of high-cost stoppages at a computer or clearing centre impacting on the process of money transmission. On the collapse of formal bargaining procedures in 1977–8, when arbitration was abandoned, this became crucial, especially as the strategy of BIFU (and ASTMS) was to try to use their bargaining power to further clerical claims. The cost for the banks in relying on domestic bargaining is their exposure to comparability claims which are extremely difficult not to concede, nevertheless, it ensures the isolation of those groups that are relatively powerful. For the unions, however, their substantial membership in the computer areas has at least probably ensured that the possibility of losing recognition — which was considered by some of the banks after the collapse of the joint staff side — has been discounted.

Overall, the management of labour at the enterprise level has not involved fundamental changes to arrangements constructed around 1970. Stability has been the central feature of the organisational arrangements as the banks have sought to balance the firm line taken on wage costs, but the counterpart to wage control concerns manning and work levels. Figure 5.1 showing the trends in employment and output demonstrates that in the 1970s the two factors were positively correlated but that since 1980 the relationship has altered significantly as the banks have tried to hold down employment levels more firmly. Overall since 1980 the employment level has been relatively stable, the drop in 1981 occurring to compensate for over-recruitment the previous year. By greater restraint on wage changes and by raising productivity through much tighter hiring policies the banks have thus been able to secure markedly greater control over their labour cost base.

Because of the automation of numerous areas of work this does not necessarily mean that effort intensification has occurred, but in some banks this has been the case. Barclays raised its work measurement standards in 1981 against which its staffing levels are fixed. Similarly, Williams and Glyn's tightened its staffing ratios after 1983 and the Midland extended its work measurement activity to get greater control over productivity. However, at the branch level all of the banks have tried to raise output per employee by substituting part-time for full-time staff, and this is discussed in more detail in the next chapter. Overall, therefore, the effort side of the employment relationship has been subject to considerable scrutiny and, significantly, manning and job standards

Figure 5.1: Indices of Employment and Output in the Banks

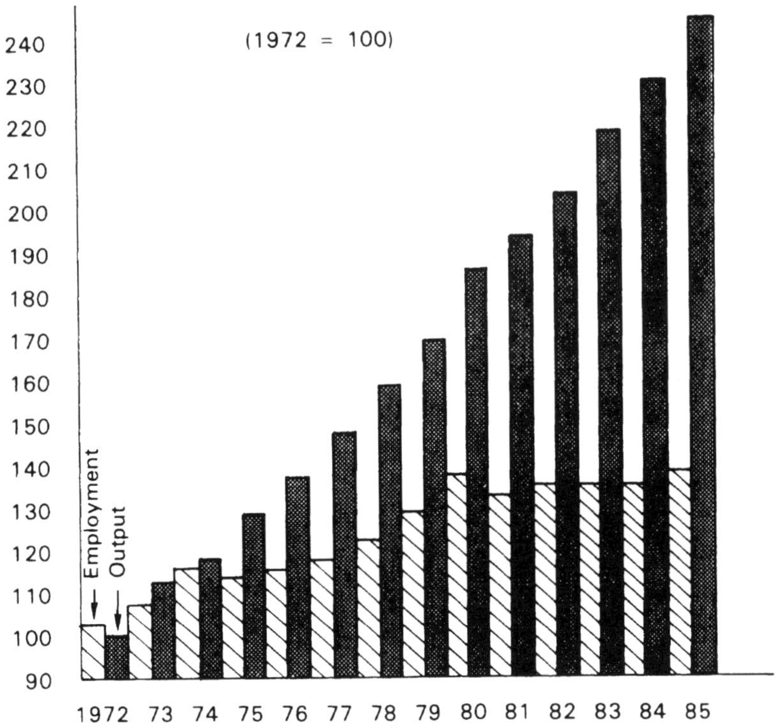

Source: CLCB + FLCBE
Note: output = items transmitted through clearing system.

have never been negotiable. This offers managers a considerable degree of freedom to raise productivity as long as the unions do not attempt to obtain some control over these issues. Hence the object of management strategy has not been to reduce trade union activity but to mould it within a general pattern of labour relations which does not inhibit organisation change, but rather makes the implementation of such change more predictable.

Conclusions

This chapter examined the responses to the growing competitiveness in banking in the area of labour relations and showed how these pressures had affected collective relationships procedurally and in substantive terms.

It also argued that a feature of recent innovations was the closer influence of the most senior levels of management on the conduct of affairs as the need to control labour costs became central to operational objectives. Additional factors precipitating this management action were the collapse of joint working between the unions and, in pay determination, what Ferner (1985) referred to as the 'permissive' environment of the recession coupled with a strong political influence. Internally, variable rates of profit and the inter-union rivalry created problems for the continuation of the employer combination and despite the apparent effectiveness of the Federation in responding to the need for a 'tougher' management approach, these internal difficulties prompted the disruption of national bargaining with the Midland's withdrawal at the end of 1985.

Until then, the two discrete levels of bargaining provided the structure through which change and stability were reconciled. At the enterprise level the maintenance of stability was paramount and was engineered by greater consultation with the unions and direct staff communications. This implied a relatively passive managerial approach but it was not necessarily incompatible with the perceived need for greater efficiency, principally because it established a suitable context in which this could be pursued through automation. This is discussed next.

6 TECHNICAL CHANGE GROWTH AND CHANGING EMPLOYMENT PATTERNS

Introduction

Throughout the period covered by this book the banks have made profound technical changes, affecting both the products or services they market and the processes by which business is transacted. Indeed, technical change has been a major catalyst to business growth and to change in the nature of competition in the finance sector as a whole (Llewellyn, 1985). It has facilitated the restructuring of markets, the diversification of firms into new and overlapping segments through innovations to the modes of distributing cash and money transmission. Unsurprisingly therefore, the banks have become major investors in technical hardware, spending substantial amounts on updating, developing or introducing data-processing systems, automatic telling machines and electronic point of sales networks which link directly from non-bank retail outlets to accounts. In 1985, Barclays stated it had commited £100m per annum to new technology purchases over the medium term and, in 1984, National Westminster indicated it would spend £600 million over five years.

Organisationally, the effects of new technology have also been profound, not least because it has facilitated the increases in productivity over the past 25 years which have enabled the banks to grow profitability in periods of high wage inflation, despite being labour-intensive businesses and in the context of rising competitive pressures. Managing the introduction of new technology has thus been central to the banks' labour strategies. Although it is beyond the scope of this book to examine the proposition that new technology has generally 'deskilled' the workforce (see Crompton and Jones, 1984; Child, 1985; Kirchner *et al.*, 1984), the nature of tasks and skills has clearly altered. Furthermore, as it has affected career progression and numbers employed, new technology has impacted upon the core factors in the traditionally co-operative employment relationship of security and upward mobility.

This chapter discusses these trends in more detail, starting with a description of the types of technical change which have been implemented. It then examines the process of managing change, demonstrating how, although the banks have consistently refused to negotiate over the strategic issues of the direction of innovation with the unions because of its centrality to competitive success, they have become more prepared to consult in order to ensure staff acceptance. Thirdly, the consequences of technical change are examined by considering trends in productivity and employment levels; finally, the implications for the structure of the banks' labour forces, which have long been organised by a dual labour market broadly based on sex are considered.

Types of Change

A dichotomy can be drawn between product and process innovations when analysing the nature and consequences of technical change (Rajan, 1984). The latter type refers to the production process, while the former refers to the outcome, the service produced for the marketplace, but banking makes this dichotomy difficult to distinguish in practical terms and thus somewhat artificial because no concrete good is produced. As Nicholas (1982) has noted, many of the products offered by the banks have changed very little in the period of technical change, rather, it is the way in which the customer gains access or transacts these products which has changed. This means that the link between changes to products and to banking processes is very close: Willman and Cowan (1984) showed, for instance, how automatic teller machines contained elements of product and process innovation to the functions of cash distribution and account information storage. Generally, product innovations affect either the method of undertaking a transaction between customers and bank or the point at which the customer enters the banking system. The use of a credit card as an automatic means of obtaining credit without a prior contact with a lending officer in a branch, or use of a cash card via a computer-terminal are examples. Clearly, such innovations have implications for the nature of competition between financial enterprises, particularly in terms of the need for a branch system to extend credit or take deposits.

Process changes have mainly been applied to the three main operational functions of the retail banks. These are: cash distribution; money transmission for deposits or lending transactions; and the storage and retrieval of account information. Process-directed innovations dominated the first wave of electromechanically-based technical change in the 1960s. These took advantage of the commercial development of large mainframe computers and allowed the centralisation of accounts records, the automation of calculation of interest and charges and the printing of customer statements. Previously, these functions had taken place within the branch on manual ledgers, and had involved the majority of clerical staff; the new computer systems took over these functions but were not originally linked on-line to the branches.

Simultaneously, automation of the labour-intensive clearing system began to transform the process of money transmission. Previously all items were collected and sorted by hand, but automated reader-sorters were introduced, using magnetic ink character recognition imprinted onto the cheques. A further innovation in 1968 to the money transmission system occurred with the development of a voucherless payment facility, the Bankers' Automated Clearing Service (BACS). Instead of exchanging paper, data-coded magnetic tapes enabled the transfer of funds to take place between banks. Apart from being a process innovation designed to reduce the amount of paper passing through the money transmission network, this was also a new product aimed at corporate customers to facilitate wage payments. It was also, therefore, a means of expanding business by encouraging the transfer away from wage payment in cash to payment into a bank account. As Cowan (1985) notes, the impact of Bankers' Automated Clearing Systems (BACS) may be judged from the tenfold increase in the number of automated payment transactions between 1969 and 1982 to 544 million. In 1985, over 800 million transactions were passed through, 22 per cent of the total clearing (IBRO).

Overall, the notable features of changes in the 1960s was that they were designed to meet increasing business volumes and overcome the logistical difficulties of a growing amount of paper vouchers in circulation, rather than to introduce radical changes to the banking service or displace labour, although this latter factor undoubtedly did occur in certain areas. Moreover, in managing change, there was a considerable degree of inter-bank co-operation and caution; the automation of the clearing system was planned by a committee of the CLCB to ensure commonality, and proceeded largely from the experience of the American banks which had pioneered change in the 1950s.

The 1970s saw what Rajan has called a second phase of technical change. A principal element of this was the completion of the automation of branch accounting with the introduction of an on-line terminal system in each of the banks' branches. Hence, all the branches were connected to the central computer in a way which allowed the direct transmission and storage of account information. Branches were also able to communicate with each other and to effect direct transfers of funds. New payment services and management information systems were then developed which, by enabling the banks to market various services to different groups, contained a product as well as a process element. The latter existed in the linking and servicing of the branch by other parts of the same organisation — such as foreign exchange dealing or trustee and tax departments and established the potential for closer control from the centre of the banks via access to branch account information.

New products included cheque cards and the credit card. The latter was first introduced by Barclays in the 1960s and represented an alternative to the use of cheques and the current account overdraft, but it did not lead to a reduction in that mode of payment and cheque volumes continued to rise, along with credit card transactions. Another major retail banking product innovation affecting cash distribution was the automatic teller machine, (ATM) which started the development of self-service banking. Initially these dispensed only cash, but the range of services has since been expanded and individual bank systems have been made compatible. At the same time, the money transmission services were being automated, both by the introduction of electronic systems of international payment, and by changes to the domestic clearing systems. In 1977 SWIFT (Society for the World Wide Inter-Bank Financial Telecommunications) began operating as an international network between banks and, in 1984, the Clearing House Automated Payments System (CHAPS) came into operation, permitting voucherless same-day settlements on larger sums.

Arguably, a third stage of development has started to occur with the objective of integrating the various data and word-processing networks operated by the banks. One result is that while computerisation was mainly concentrated on the back office in the past, now it is being extended to the points at which customers and their bank come into contact. One result is the use of visual display units, installed to provide information on which lending and marketing decisions can be made. This can be seen as a novel form of process innovation going beyond the traditional functions of cash and payments transmission. Cashiers can obtain direct contact to information storage systems through counter-terminals, which will increasingly perform security checks formerly done manually. The banks are also installing mini-computer networks which permit the decentralisation of decisions about the way accounting records are stored and facilitate the process of risk assessments on which lending decisions are made. Midland has installed Nixdorf computers and National Westminster used Burroughs machines linked to IBM mainframe models for this purpose. Mini-computers can also be used in specialised functions such as credit card departments for the authorisation of transactions.

Other extensions of the automation of payment transactions are currently in their infancy, but promise to bring about profound reforms to the industry. These include the making of payments through credit cards inserted into the point of sale machines which transfer funds direct from a customer's account by electronic signal and without the exchange of vouchers. Another is the extension of shopping and payment points from customers' homes, through their own computers. A mixture of technical, legal, financial and marketing factors has thus far impeded the rapid growth of these networks. However, predicted trends suggest they will expand in the 1990s (Marti and Zeilinger, 1982).

Competitive Effects

There is little doubt that new technology has been a crucial competitive stimulus. From the 1960s, automation allowed cost-effective growth in the banking industry to occur by providing an efficient means of payment-processing. More recently, it has broken down the barriers between different parts of the finance sector; hence the proposals for the reform of the clearing system made by the Child Committee (1984) were explicitly based on the 'recent developments in technology'. In particular, the growth of automated money transmission systems and voucherless payment methods has allowed what were previously non-clearing bank intermediaries to operate more like clearers. Additionally, it has been seen that new technology has facilitated new products and services which allowed the banks to market themselves to new customers. An example is the changing range of payment methods for salaries, which are broken down by usage in Table 6.1. But on the other hand, because the entry points to the financial system have been changed, the banks are no longer necessary parties to certain types of transaction, where previously they held a monopoly: the introduction of credit cards by large retail stores is an example. In the foreign exchange markets, the growth of international telecommunications has led to a proliferation of competing banks. Indeed, the treasury departments of many large companies also effectively act like banks by having access to market information upon which they can manage their currency transactions. This is achieved by direct linkages to the data bases of banks.

Secondly, there is a blurring of industry demarcations whereby the functions of banks and, say, supermarkets will increasingly overlap as automatic teller machines are located away from branches, and possibly serviced by non-bank staff. Yet, on the other hand, the banks may move

Table 6.1: Wage and Salary Payment Methods

	1976	1981	1984
	%	%	%
Cash	58	42	37
Cheque	12	15	16
Giro credit	26	38	43
Not known	4	5	4

into other financial services such as the capital markets, where additional functions are put through their existing networks, therby reducing fixed costs per transaction. Thirdly, new telecommunications networks allow foreign as well as domestic competition to proliferate, reducing the degree of domestic protection enjoyed previously by the clearers.

As a result, the overlap in the financial sector has accelerated. The banks' move into long-term household finance is an example of their expansionary programmes while, in contrast, the American-owned Citibank has expanded by acquisition of a stake in the credit card Diners Club UK, in a merchant bank and a London insurance broker, and provides an electronic banking service for corporate customers. Increasingly, the intention is to provide a financial service package based on these kinds of linkages between different parts of the sector.

One important effect on the clearing banks' domestic divisions has concerned their branch structures. Formerly these were the central element of competition and growth, but technological innovation has altered their value as a means of gathering deposits and new customers. In short, there is simply less need to maintain or staff such expensive networks in the traditional manner. Branches will thus be turned over more to the processing of ancillary services like insurance and to marketing of the banks' products (Frazer and Vittas, 1982). One consequence is that the existing security windows dividing customers from offices will be removed and more space given over to selling in an open-plan environment.

As a first stage of reform, all the clearers have pursued some degree of branch segmentation. This means that the branch systems are reorganised and individual branch functions defined more closely by market requirements. Such change is facilitated by technical innovations which permit more flexible account storage and retrieval, and greater discretion over the format of information retained. Yet while all the banks are reducing the size of their branch networks, a degree of choice on the desired structure exists. Barclays has gone furthest down the road in trying to develop a three-tier system, and by 1985 was halfway through its programme (Turner, 1985). Its key branches servicing corporate clients will number about 150, with about 1,700 mid-size branches offering a range of services for smaller commercial customers and private accounts. About 500 further branches will effectively operate as money shops, providing a small range of ancillary services as well.

The logic is both cost and market based: account-processing and managerial expertise will both be concentrated and distributed more according to demand. Similarly, Midland began to segment its branch structure around 1980, setting up local 'lead' offices where operations were centralised and concentrating its corporate banking on area offices. Midland also began to rationalise its branch structure more radically under pressure of comparatively high overhead costs and increasing debts, closing 200 between 1980 and 1985, whereas it was only latterly that National Westminster began its segmentation strategy, having initially pursued a highly-structured configuration in pilot exercises of a leading branch with several satellites and then abandoned this in favour of a less formalised model. None the less, in the medium term the bank will, like Barclays, establish about 150 corporate branches and a number of operational centres, while closing up to 100 branches and downgrading 800 more. In contrast, Lloyds has displayed the greatest continuity in its branch organisation, avoiding large-scale change after a small pilot exercise examined the principles of this approach in the early 1970s. It has, however, decentralised its lending and marketing functions at the local level somewhat. Clearly, these changes have been driven by the combination of market 'pull' and technological 'push' factors, which are closely interlinked, and they have consequences for employment levels, and the management of labour relations which are examined below.

The Management of Change

In the implementation of new technology, the fundamental objective of the banks has been to sustain unilateral control over the decision-making process while maintaining the consent of their employees to change and the need for it. This has required a number of key decisions in the area of labour management regarding the scope, level and style of joint negotiation, and represents the strongest test to their co-operative labour relations system.

Perhaps the fundamental advantage for the banks has been the non-deleterious effect, thus far, on employment and careers of technical change. It has not therefore conflicted with the traditional bases of the banks' labour strategies; indeed, to the extent that it facilitated business growth it enhanced the opportunities for progression and job security. For these reasons the move to branch computerisation in the late 1960s was welcomed by the staff bodies at the time on the tacit understanding that no job loss would result, and the same was true of the automation of the clearing centres. Management arguments that new technology would upgrade the skill levels of the workforce were also a factor favouring acceptance of change, it being assumed that it would be the boring and repetitive sorting jobs in the cheque-clearing process that would be eliminated. However, this is not to suggest that change was negotiated in any way; at that time the union was struggling for recognition and the associations saw such an issue as outside the scope of joint determination.

Even after recognition, when NUBE and the associations were working jointly, there was no negotiation over change. Again, automation was associated with job gains and this growth was one of the reasons for the unfettered managerial control of new technology. Another was that as neither the national union nor the associations had any tradition of work-place control or negotiation they could not have controlled the actual implementation of technical change closely.

A firmer line emerged from BIFU, however, when the joint staff side collapsed and more overt competition for members began. This coincided with a less benign view emerging in the union over the consequences of new technology. BIFU began to express concern over the poorer prospects for employment and with the potential for a reduction in skills inherent in technical change (BIFU, 1980–1982). At the same time its strategy of forcing the associations to compete in the bargaining process to demonstrate their putative ineffectiveness dictated that BIFU should try to widen the scope of negotiations and its area of influence. Also coinciding with this were the first signs of the banks responding to the increasingly competitive product market by proposals to stem the growth in labour costs. The increasingly tough position on pay negotiations was one element of this policy; revised opening hours, automation of cash distribution, extension of voucherless payment transactions and the segmentation of the branch structures were others. For the first time the banks were confronted with union demands for joint control over the introduction of new technology just when industrial action seemed more likely due to inter-union competition and they themselves were trying to increase the pace of change.

At this point the banks had to make choices over the level and scope of any negotiations on new technology. Although systems differences existed between them, one option was for a national agreement which established that technical change was negotiable and broadly sought adjustment along the lines favoured by BIFU through reductions in hours of work. The Federation directorate proposed such a national framework on the grounds that it would provide the best guarantee against the threat of disruption but still offer autonomy at the enterprise level to determine the detailed direction and pace of innovation. In effect, while this implied a sharing of power, this would be limited by the multi-level bargaining structure. No individual bank could accept such a devolution of power away from the enterprise however, and despite the acknowledged risk of union action, each was loathe to be committed to a formal acceptance of joint control, as ideologically unacceptable and too risky in terms of limiting potential commercial advantage. Admittedly, in the Midland, where BIFU was the majority union and faced no staff association and where management had pursued a more accommodating policy since the mid-1970s, a job security agreement was signed in 1980 but as it did not reduce working hours or guarantee no redundancies, nor incorporate a full joint decision-making process for technical innovation, this was a marked dilution of the union's demands. The bank did agree to try to minimise any job loss through transfers and retraining, however, which was more than BIFU was able to obtain elsewhere, the other banks declining to sign any formal agreement. Subsequently, National Westminster signed a similar agreement with its association, which again simply offered consultation over any job implications of proposed changes, rather than an area of joint decision-making but because of the inter-union competition in this bank, BIFU was hostile to this agreement and would not be party to it.

In trying to gain influence over the decision-making process, the unions faced the further problem that the input from the personnel function in each of the banks was limited. Child and Tarbuck's case study (1985) emphasised that the key planning and policy matters were the responsibility of the Management Services Department (MSD), which then made recommendations direct to the most senior policy committees in the bank. These authors concluded that:

> The MSD . . . has operated as a technical elite both in respect of its influence and exclusivity in the process . . . The possiblities for direct trade union influence in this decision process are thus clearly limited by its centralisation and by the driving role of a highly informed technical department. (p.7)

It is also because the banks take a broadly optimistic view of the staff response to change that they have not felt it necessary to concede to demands for the negotiation of the terms of change. This optimism is based largely on what is assumed to be its job-enriching potential. None the less, localised experience of staff discontent with certain changes in the past, such as the branch satelliting project in National Westminster, and the desire to sustain a high degree of staff good will, has expanded the previously marginal role of the personnel function. This in turn has presented the opportunity for further union influence. Prior to implementation, the unions are now informed of proposed changes which are likely to affect a significant number of staff, such as the introduction of counter-terminals, and are now involved in the monitoring of pilot exercises which are themselves more extended. National Westminster and the Midland, for example, both sought extensive discussions with the unions in the extensions of their mini-computer networks in the branches involving them in discussions of trials, the shape of piloting exercises, monitoring the results and staff reaction and circulating information on projected staffing levels and grade changes. Union proposals led in one case to amendments to decisions on the timing of the introduction of a network, as well as the proposed reorganisation of tasks.

For the banks there are recognised to be certain advantages in extending joint consultation. Not only does this minimise the risks of staff resistance to new technology, but it augments the management reporting systems which, in such centralised large organisations, tend to be over-extended. Several personnel managers admitted the unions were frequently 'closer to the ground' and gave a more accurate account of what staff views were to senior managers in charge of directing the pace of change. This short-circuiting of the system has also enhanced the standing of personnel departments, which were then able to expand their influence in the management of change. The aims of the personnel departments and the trade unions have thus worked in a mutually reinforcing way to moderate the technical supremacy of the MSD.

However, the degree of control the unions can obtain has also been limited. This has been achieved by the case-by-case approach to change which, although allowing consultation to shade into negotiation to a certain extent, has not meant the employers have had to concede formally any rights of negotiation over technical change. They can still ultimately define the limits to what is negotiable or even open to joint discussion. This means union influence is focused heavily on the application stage of innovation rather than earlier parts of the process, and therefore does not impinge upon strategic decisions over the rationale for change and its broad direction.

In other cases, it has been localised staff resistance which has allowed the unions, and particularly BIFU, to extend their influence. In Lloyds staff opposition to technical change in its Jersey branches in 1983 led to disruption and resulted in a local technology agreement with BIFU which provided for extensive consultation and retraining as well as firmer guarantees on job security. In the Midland in 1984 a dispute developed in the Blackpool area over branch restructuring plans; in this instance BIFU was able to obtain a moratorium from the bank and a revision of the satelliting proposals.

Other disputes have also occurred as particular groups have been affected by technical change: in 1985, messengers in National Westminster's City of London area took action over the threat of redundancy from the automation of the payment system; the disruption of shift patterns among data-processing and engineering staff in the computer centres has also been a source of disputes. These have not been major stoppages, but they have tended to contribute to the more active role of the personnel function in moderating the technicist policies of the Management Services Departments.

None the less the direction and parameters of change are still unilaterally set by senior management because new technology applications are so close to the central business objectives of the banks and to the achievement of productivity growth. The area of joint agreement over change is thus bound to be limited and, for this reason, the banks are very unlikely to concede to the basic demand that BIFU has put forward to share the benefits of new technology by a reduction in the standard working week, conflicting as it does with the fundamental aim of reducing labour costs while sustaining business growth.

Employment Effects

Thus far technical innovation in banking has not been associated with falling employment levels. Certainly, jobs have been displaced or altered by process changes, as for example in the clearing system where Child and Tarbuck (1985) quoted a rise in productivity in their case-study of one clearer of 62 per cent between 1970 and 1982. However, product changes resulting from new technology have tended to have the opposite effect in raising the demand for bank products and indirectly raising the banks' factor demand. As was illustrated above, and is also argued by Rajan (1984), product and process changes are in practice so closely linked that process changes designed to save labour tend to have a stimulating effect via new product demand at the same time and thus far the overall employment rate associated with technical change has been positive. This is true of the banking sector as a whole and for the clearing banks in particular (see Table 1.2).

Other surveys suggest that future prospects are mixed. Rajan (1984) predicted a rise of between 5 and 10 per cent in employment in the banking industry as a whole and the clearing banks specifically between 1983 and 1988 — a simple annual growth of 1–2 per cent; a similarly optimistic outlook was taken by Robertson *et al.* (1982). A survey of the Scottish banks expected growth until the mid-1980s to be followed by a plateau in employment levels in the latter part of the decade (Gaskin and Gaskin, 1980), giving a 10 per cent drop between 1980–90 and Shaw and Coulbeck (1983) predicted a 12 per cent loss from the effects of automation alone in British banking over the same period. Evidently, even if some growth in employment may still be expected, the rate of expansion is decreasing and is likely to reach a plateau in the short to medium term.

Such predictions will inevitably be problematic, but three of the main factors affecting the level of employment may be considered here briefly. The first is the rate of business growth which in turn is a function of a number of complex factors, including the rate of growth in the economy as a whole, and the degree of competitive success achieved by the other financial services institutions. In terms of business growth, Shaw and Coulbeck (1983) see this sustained until 1990 by (*inter alia*) the increase in wages paid by cheque or direct transfer to current account in substitution for cash. This trend remains difficult to predict precisely however: the Inter-Bank Research Organisation expected the account-holding population to rise by about 5 per cent between 1986 and 1991, but noted that future cheque volumes are more volatile, being dependent on the progress made with Electronic Funds Transfer (EFT), and could either fall by 0.5 billion or rise by up to 6 billion in the same period. From the banks' point of view, they remain confident that growth will continue, although the market is increasingly competitive. Most specifically, one bank suggested a medium-term rate of growth of 4–5 per cent per annum in business, which is in line with recent performance.

Secondly, branch restructuring has to be considered. Current changes in the branch systems are broad-ranging, but the reshaping process is not a new phenomenon. Branch numbers have been falling since the bank amalgamations of the late 1960s, dropping by 9 per cent between 1968 and 1980. A recent management consultancy prediction that 5 per cent of branches would close between 1983 and 1990 thus does not seem so exceptional. On the other hand, the reorganising principle which seeks to centralise functions on one local lead branch is novel, and as has been argued throughout this book, the existing branch organisations represented a mode of competition which reached its peak 20 years ago and are now increasingly outdated. Yet they represent a considerable capital investment which could not be quickly disposed of so that the actual rate of change in the branch structure is unlikely to be as fast as technical change would allow (Frazer and Vittas, 1982).

Furthermore managers are unwilling to contemplate shedding large numbers of staff compulsorily because of the deteriorating effect this is assumed to have on organisational commitment and co-operation with change. Hence adjustment strategies have been developed involving the redeployment of clerical staff into other functions and departments. Evidence from the Midland illustrates this. It has shed some 8,000 jobs since 1980 but avoided large-scale redundancy by redeployment to other departments; only 10 per cent of the staff involved were made redundant. This process is obviously facilitated by the natural wastage of the sizeable number of female staff in their twenties and only 100 of the redundancies were compulsory. Thus, while the banks no longer rule job loss out and have introduced redundancy procedures to deal with this, the combination of natural wastage and the paternalistic ethos has led them to avoid abrupt adjustments to the product market.

Thirdly, the nature and pace of innovation has to be taken into account. Although large capital investment is taking place, there are grounds for arguing that the next major changes in retail banking remain some way off. These changes concern the spread of home banking and of the Electronic Funds Transfer, Point of Sales (EFTPOS) schemes. Consumer resistance is said to impede the diffusion of the former scheme and disagreements with retailers about the ownership and sharing of investment costs have impeded the latter. A trial network for EFTPOS is being implemented once more by the banks, but by 1990 only 10 per cent of the total cheque volumes are expected to be displaced by this system (CIS, 1983).

In the shorter term, the growing number of ATMs represents a potentially greater displacement factor. Table 6.2 shows the rising number of these machines in the big four banks. According to Rajan (1984), ten ATMs provided a saving of seven staff, although BIFU believes the figure is much higher, at around twenty staff (BIFU, 1985). Using Rajan's calculation, between 1981–5 some 2,335 jobs were displaced by ATMs. However, the survey of ATM installations in a retail bank carried out by Willman and Cowan (1984) brought out the point that staff savings were highly contingent on branch business, volumes of transactions and locations. The authors suggested little consideration was given to staffing factors in the decisions over cost effectiveness and that in some cases ATM installations created work increases. A senior Barclays manager has also stated that ATM installations, although labour-saving, did generate more enquiries per customer than had been the norm with cashier transactions thereby increasing expected costs (Nicholas, 1982).

Table 6.2: ATMs in the Banks

ATMS	1981		1983		1985	
B	NCR		NCR 1,770		NCR 1,770	
	770		1,773		1,773	
	1,780	207	1,780	591	1,780	807
			IBM 3,624		5,070	
					5,080	
					IBM 3,624	
L	IBM 2,984		IBM 2,984		IBM 2,984	
	3,614		3,614		3,614	
	3,624		3,624		3,624	
		1,109		1,483		1,672
M	NCR 1,780		NCR 1,780		NCR 1,770	
					1,780	
					5,080	
					1,773	
		193		597		922
NW	NCR 770		NCR 770		NCR 1,770	
	1,780		1,770			
			1,780			
			5,080			
		341		874		1,784
TOTAL		1,850		3,545		5,185

Source: *The Banker* (1981–5); Rajan (1984)

Furthermore, the application of technical innovation tends to be highly incremental in practice and the savings from a new piece of equipment or reorganisation of tasks may often not amount to a full-time employee at the micro-level. For instance, a change proposed by the organisation and methods department of one bank would have meant a total saving of 42 staff spread through the whole domestic division and was therefore rejected as unworthwhile. Perhaps the incremental nature of much technical change at the branch level helps to explain why bank staff have not generally seen new technology as a threat to jobs. It means, as well, that the productivity gains from new technology tend to be marginal in the short run, except where part-time staff can be substituted for full-time.

This suggests that total employment levels may well be relatively unresponsive to technical or organisational change in the medium term.

Taking the banking sector as a whole, Rajan (1984) pointed out that increases in staffing have decelerated in each decade since 1960, when technical innovation started. In the clearing banks the rise in employment was rapid until 1980, but Figure 5.1 showed how output has risen much faster than employment over the past decade or so and that increasingly large business growth is necessary before employment growth is generated. Here the output basis is the number of transactions per annum passed through the inter-branch clearing. As Frazer (1982) noted, this indicator of physical productivity cannot control for the change in bank business over time which may alter the nature of the 'product', but its value lies in the fact that about 60 per cent of total staff are involved in payment transmission.

The argument that the growth rates of previous years in employment will not be repeated seems likely to be borne out. Rajan's prediction of a growth rate of around 1 per cent per annum for the banking sector to 1987 thus far seems accurate for, although employment grew by 9.3 per cent from the beginning of 1980 to the end of 1984, the figure drops to 5.8 per cent if part-time jobs are taken as half an employee. The one bank which would reveal its projections envisaged an increase in numbers of new jobs of 1.5 per cent per annum to the end of the decade. The majority of these would be part-time, however, and this was contingent upon business growth of 4–5 per cent per annum.

Other banks have similar projections for productivity, but the expected industry average is perhaps lower than the above figure. In effect, then, staff increases are dependent upon minimal rises in business volumes of 2–3 per cent per annum. In the case of the bank quoted above, the expected increase in jobs was around 1,000 per annum in the short term, slowing to 500 by 1989. Extrapolating this trend would give a total of between 235,000 and 240,000 staff by the end of the decade for the clearing banks as a whole.

Qualitative Changes in the Banks' Workforce

Despite the long growth in employment, the effects of new technology, coupled with the response of the banks to rising competition, have already started to affect the nature of work and careers and will increasingly do so. Kirchner (1984) predicts, for example, that while clerical jobs like cashiering and voucher-processing are likely to be reduced by ATMs and counter-terminals, computer and data-processing related jobs are likely to rise. Rajan saw similar trends, and Crompton and Jones (1984) predicted a further stratification of the workforce as centralisation of control and decentralisation of function are facilitated by automation. In other words, clerical work is increasingly routinised and 'degraded' (quite literally), while a smaller number of elite staff attain senior positions. All of which suggests as well that female employment, which is concentrated in the lower clerical grades, will be disproportionately affected by technical change, both through displacement and reduced prospects for grade progression.

The evidence reveals a more complex picture than might be assumed, however. Undoubtedly the clerical functions are changing and will be affected by automation but, as Kirchner (1984) indicated, the impact of autommation is not invariably to reduce clerical jobs and, as the profiles of clerical employment levels given in Table 6.3 show, the impact of new technology is still working though. For example, other things being equal, one might expect managerial posts to be falling for two reasons. First, although the number of branches has been falling slowly since 1970, satelliting is likely to reduce more quickly the number of managerial posts as the secondary and tertiary levels are downgraded and run by appointed supervisiory staff. Secondly, the introduction of credit scoring allows the delegation of the lending function to senior clerical staff. Thus far, however, although the number of branches is falling in each bank, the only reduction in full management posts has taken place in the Midland, and elsewhere the number has expanded. This growth may be explained by the trend towards specialisation of managerial functions and the expansion of divisional and corporate bureaucracies.

Table 6.3: Grade Numbers, Selected Years

	76		81		84	
		%		%		%
Grade 1	32,612	18.8	27,347	15.1	25,826	14.0
2	64,635	37.2	64,829	35.8	62,061	33.5
3	26,151	15.0	31,341	17.2	34,835	18.8
4	14,128	8.1	16,113	8.9	18,572	10.0
4+	21,621	12.4	24,429	13.5	26,004	14.1
Man	14,726	8.5	17,248	9.5	17,835	9.6
Total	173,873	100.0	181,334	100.0	185,133	100.0

Source: London clearing banks

There has also been an expansion of senior clerical and supervisory posts. Part of the explanation for this increase appears to lie in the move into lending and marketing duties by these staff. Barclays has gone further done this road than its competitors, creating 600 customer account officers from its Grade 3 staff in 1984–5 specifically to sell the bank's services within the branches. But the other banks have also expanded the proportion of senior clerical positions. This trend is associated with the restructuring of the branch systems and the delegation of lending and marketing tasks to these groups demonstrating how strategic decisions on the degree of restructuring and task reorganisation adopted in the future are thus likely to be significant determinants of the grade structure of each bank. Senior managers also suggested that not only is the senior clerical job changing in content, but that much of the recent increase in business has been shouldered there. In contrast, the data on the junior grades covering the machinists and the cashiering work indicate the effects of product and process innovation most clearly. Numbers have fallen both absolutely and proportionately but have been held up to an extent by increasing business volumes. Otherwise one might have expected a much larger fall due to the displacement effects of ATMs and counter-terminals which allow remittances and customer enquiries to be keyed in to the computer by the cashier directly, rather than being passed to the back office for processing.

The employment of women in banking is closely tied up with trends in clerical employment, because in the post-war period the banks have employed them as a secondary labour force occupying lower level jobs with less career progression. In Chapter 3 it was shown how female employment expanded with the growth in banking employment and as the supply of male staff became tighter. That they were paid on different age-scales which widened after the mid-twenties in favour of men, indicated how males moved into more senior positions on the assumption that they were preparing for a managerial career, while females were retained in more routine positions. Female employees increased proportionately to males from the 1950s onwards (see Table 6.4) and by the end of 1984 there were 139,352 (58 per cent) women in London clearing banks' employment, and 99,617 men (source: CLCB).

Yet in some respects the banks' employment practices did not fit the classic dual labour market model which was predicated upon a differentiation in conditions of work *and* opportunities between primary and secondary segments (Doeringer and Piore, 1971). The banks were formally committed to policies of equality of opportunity in the 1970s and the inferior female pay structure was abandoned. Technical innovation abolished many of the jobs in the 'factory' clearing centres where a large proportion of women were employed. At the same time certain and

Table 6.4: Proportion of Females Employed in the Banks

	Females (%)
1959	40
1965	48
1970	53
1976	55
1978	56
1980	58
1982	58
1985	59

paternalist practices such as the expectation that women would resign on marriage, also died out. Exclusive reliance on internal promotion and training meant all males and females were recruited into the same entry grade (except subsequently for graduates) and rates of pay were the same within each grade for those appraised as future managerial stock and those who were not. Formally at least, equality of opportunity replaced the overt discrimination previously practised.

However, women have continued to be less likely to reach managerial or supervisory ranks. Table 6.5 showing the proportion of women in the clerical and managerial grades of the London clearers, illustrates the concentration in the lower grades. Within the general picture some inter-bank variations are evident, as is shown in Table 6.6, which compares Barclays — with a higher proportion of females in each grade — with National Westminster, but the overall structure of female employment in each shows a decline after the junior clerical grades. A further marginal change over the last decade is that the proportion of women in senior clerical and supervisory grades has risen throughout the period, while that of the most junior grades has fallen slightly. A small rise in the proportion of managers who are women has also occurred, although this is still under 2 per cent of the total managerial population. In absolute terms the rise is much more significant for, as Povall (1985) shows, the number of women managers in 1978 was 197 and five years later the figure was 328.

Table 6.5: Proportion of Females by Grade, London Clearers

	1976	1981	1985
Grade 1	75.3	74.5	68.9
2	75.5	76.6	77.7
3	53.9	61.0	67.2
4	24.6	27.6	33.0
4+	7.8	13.5	16.7
Man.	1.3	1.5	2.4

Source: Clearing banks

Table 6.6: Workforce Composition, Two Banks 1976 and 1984

	1976					1984			
	B		NW			B		NW	
	Nos. in grade	% female	Nos. in grade	% female		Nos. in grade	% female	Nos. in grade	% female
1	7,678	80.7	9,627	72.6	1	7,824	74.5	9,248	66.9
2	15,558	79.9	16,786	71.87	2	15,048	85.0	20,459	74.5
3	6,754	64.7	5,914	47.9	3	12,047	78.1	8,162	62.2
4	3,144	33.7	3,870	14.4	4	4,165	46.9	6,219	30.8
4+	6,340	9.1	6,645	6.17	4+	8,055	20.3	8,577	13.1
M	4,102	2.12	4,352	1.05	M	6,299	2.8	5,068	1.6

Given that their policies were based upon equality of opportunity, the banks have explained the sexual variation in career performance primarily in terms of difference in attitudes and ambition. Other work suggested that employer discrimination in pre-entry qualifications was contributory (Povall *et al.*, 1982), and this was linked to a bias in policy regarding the acquisition of post-entry qualifications which were becoming increasingly important to promotion to managerial rank in the 1970s. In effect, while human capital differences between the sexes appeared to explain variations in career progression, these were themselves partly the result of employer policies (Egan, 1982).

Indeed, to operate the strong internal labour markets which permit promotion only from within the enterprise and to sustain high career opportunities, the banks arguably require a high fall-out of staff before the career path becomes fully operational. This is understood if it is remembered that clerical grades (Grades 1–4) constitute about 70 per cent of total clerical/managerial staff, but full management posts constitute only 10.6 per cent of full-time non-manual jobs (excluding data-processing staff). Thus promotion opportunities are limited even given the record of growth in business. Yet, until recently, management grades were achieved by up to 50 per cent of the male staff who stayed with a single bank throughout their working lives. This can only be achieved by wastage from the clerical grades. Indeed, wastage allows the banks to offer some promotion prospects to nearly all of their staff whilst at the same time permitting further recruitment at the port of entry to the internal labour market (Grade 1) and while keeping employment to the appropriate levels. In this sense, the static picture of the proportions of staff in each grade gives a misleading representation of how the career system operates, by failing to illustrate the timing and extent of the labour turnover. Marsden (1982) has examined this process in one clearing bank and shown that the majority of female and male quits occur when these staff are in their early to mid-twenties, when they will have reached only Grades 2 or 3.

However, the data shown in Table 6.5 suggested a greater proportion of women are occupying more senior clerical positions. This may, in part, reflect higher participation among women in the wider working population. It may partly reflect the changing quality of the female workforce as a whole, with the rising proportion of women graduates, leading to a larger number being employed by the banks, as Povall (1985) suggests. Such trends would also be enhanced by the management policies the banks have adopted to retain and promote more women into senior grades. These have originated partly from management beliefs that the turnover of women was a drain on the labour force quality, even if it facilitated the smooth operation of the internal labour market and enabled them to manage peaks and troughs in business volume or changes in quit rates (the unexpectedly low turnover in 1981 being one example of this). Partly, as well, the more reformist management view in favour of encouraging greater female occupation of senior positions has emerged from external stimuli including changes in the law, and pressure from BIFU, academic consultant bodies and organisations such as the Equal Opportunities Commission. For instance, National Westminster appointed a Career Planning Adviser in 1980 and issued new guidelines and developed a training programme for assessing and managing career progression for those women with strong management potential. A re-entry/reservist scheme was also set up to encourage the re-employment of women at their existing grade level if they left to have a child and these innovations were promoted by the bank's senior personnel manager after advice and analysis by an external specialist. Other banks have also subsequently adopted similar reservist schemes.

But these policies concentrate on the development of managerial stock from a minority of exceptionally qualified females. Many of these are graduate entrants who move on to the management development programmes after induction and initial training and appraisal, and in recent years each of the banks has been successful in increasing the proportion and number of women on these schemes: in Lloyd's, for example, between 1980 and 1983 the number rose from 107 to 240 (8.4 to 15.3 per cent) (Povall, 1985). The proportion of females recruited into management grades from the general intake of school-leavers remains small, however: in Barclays only 5 per cent of those entering the management development programme in 1984 through internal transfer were female. The policies do not, therefore, resolve the broader sexual segmentation of the workforce.

Indeed, other elements of the banks' policies have been criticised for sustaining certain disadvantages of females in secondary jobs without management career potential. In 1985 both Barclays and the Midland came under scrutiny from the EOC, the former as a result of a decision by the EOC itself and the latter via a complaint of discrimination against female staff by ASTMS. In both cases the recruitment and mobility policies have been at the heart of alleged discrimination.

There is also evidence that a more general restructuring of the workforces and career opportunities is occurring through the refinement of selection and promotion systems to produce a more formalised three-tier structure of staffing. At the bottom level are 16-year-old entrants whose expectations of progression are limited to the senior clerical and supervisory grades, and this currently includes the majority of female entrants. Above them, A-level entrants and some graduates may expect to reach low to mid-ranking branch management positions, if they are suitably appraised and achieve post-entry qualifications. At the top, a number of 'high-fliers', mainly recruited as university graduates, may expect to reach executive positions. Each of these groups has quite different career paths and work experience.

The greater segmentation is supported by more refined appraisal systems. Each of the banks tiers its staff in the initial years of employment based on performance reports and pre- and post-entry qualifications. This tiering effectively determines the career potential of the employee and thus is a strong factor in establishing promotion rates. Periodic reassessments do take place but the level of qualifications on entry and the aptitude shown in early employment are strongly associated with long-term career expectations. It is also notable that the banks are tending to turn away from giving equal encouragement to their staff to take their bankers examinations: certain clearers have already limited study-leave to top-tier entrants, while the remainder have to study in their leisure time. In effect, therefore, career progression increasingly depends on formal qualifications and the demonstration of commitment and aptitude early in employment, in contrast to the old emphasis upon experience and extended acquaintance with the range of clerical tasks.

However, it should be emphasised that the refined staffing and promotion structures which the banks are developing affect males as well as females. Furthermore, this is not an entirely new phenomenon, for as has been emphasised, it was only through the turnover of both male and female staff in their teens and early twenties that the males remaining in employment above the age of 25 could expect a high (+50 per cent) chance of attaining managerial rank. Crompton and Jones (1984) similarly concluded that career progression to management for the minority was dependent upon truncated career paths or turnover among the majority.

Insofar as it concerns the increasing use of part-time labour, females are disproportionately affected by one key part of this restructuring process. For the banks (and other employers), part-time work is a means of responding in a cost-effective way to fluctuations in business demands, and as a labour intensive service industry this effectively means varying the staffing levels to meet customers needs. For instance, part-time staff are increasingly used to cover lunch-time and other busy periods for cashiers. This allows full-time staff levels to be kept to a minimum. Figure 6.1 shows the growing number of part-timers over the past five years and illustrates the contrast with the trend in full-time employment which has fallen in the same period. Now, in terms of the sexual stratification of the labour force it is significant that the overwhelming majority of part-time workers are female, usually in the second phase of employment after starting a family. Indeed, by 1984 part-time females outnumbered full-time females by a ratio of 7:5 in the over-30 age bracket, and Rajan (1984) has gone as far as predicting that future growth in female employment will be almost entirely associated with trends in part-time work. In terms of workforce stratification, it is also notable that these part-time jobs are largely clustered in the two lowest grades (see Table 6.7) and given that the strategy of part-time employment is to respond to fluctuating customer demand for clerical services (cashiering, for example), it is predictable that the promotion opportunities for this group will remain low. At the same time, given the higher female turnover and that the areas of work most susceptible to automation are located in the lower clerical grades where females are concentrated, the proportion of full-time females will decrease in the future. To that extent the sexual stratification of bank staff is likely to be sustained.

Table 6.7: Part-time/Full-time Staff by Grade

	B		L		M		NW	
	81	84	81	84	81	84	81	84
1	33.9	27.6	6.7	4.6	7.8	7.6	14.2	13.1
2	21.1	29.6	8.5	16.9	2.0	1.5	11.2	12.2
3	2.3	2.2	0.2	0.3	0.4	0.34	0.8	0.3
4	0.5	0.5	0.05	0.05	0.09	0.04	0.1	0.1
4+	0.1	0.2	–	–	–	–	0.01	0.01
M	–	–	–	–	–	–	–	–

Figure 6.1: Part-time and Full-time Employment in the Clearing Banks

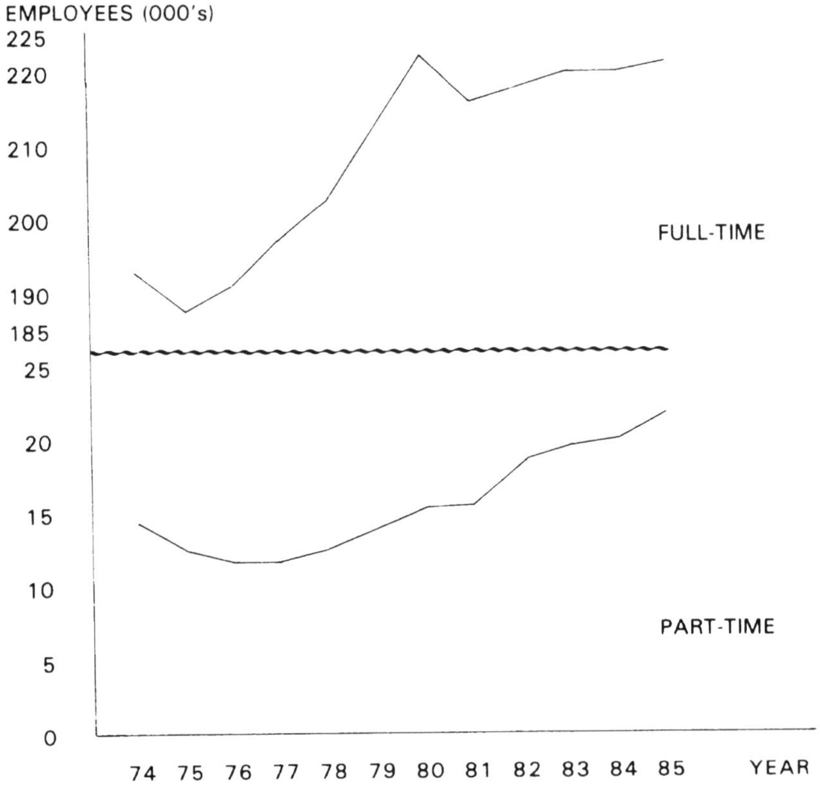

Source: CLCB Statistical Unit

Evidently, the restructuring of the labour force involves certain conflicting trends. On the one hand, opportunities for some women to progress are increasing as a result of deliberate employer policies; furthermore there is evidence of some recent policies designed to accomodate the bimodal pattern of female employment and these factors suggest that the traditional sexually-based dual labour market has been modified somewhat. Notwithstanding this, though, female employment is concentrated disproportionately in the lower clerical grades and thus susceptible to displacement through technical change. Moreover, the recent trend to raising part-time employment levels appears to be one significant factor which will sustain the secondary role of women in the banks' internal labour markets.

Conclusions

Looking at technical innovations in the banks over the past 20 years, the significant factor appears to have been its association with growing employment. This was explained in terms of the dual product and process effect of most applications, so that although labour was displaced and jobs changed, the banks have in the past been able to benefit from rising demand and the opportunity to introduce new services to offset actual job loss. The rise in employment has slowed, however, and now appears to have almost reached a plateau, as the product market reaches maturity and the displacement effects of process changes upon jobs become greater. However, it was argued that automation has gone as far as possible in some areas — such as accounting records — and that in terms of cash distribution the displacement effects were thus far dubious. Thus branch reorganisation and the growing substitution of voucherless payments through BACS for cheques may well hold the key to the rate of productivity growth and employment levels. In the longer term, much depends on the rate of penetration of other electronic payment methods (EFTPOS) and of the competitive success of the clearers.

Technical change has also influenced the structure of the banks' workforces, through its influence upon the branch structure. Some evidence exists that lower-grade clerical jobs, in which women are concentrated, are most susceptible to automation, but it was shown that more women are reaching the higher clerical grades and managerial rank. The segmentation of the banks' workforces formerly based on a relatively simple dual structure of career and non-career staff and based on sex thus appears to be growing more complex. This was associated with internal and external reformist pressure and with increasingly complex appraisal schemes which segregate staff into three or more categories for different career paths. Finally, it was noted that a feature of employment in the 1980s has been the growing number of part-timers, most of whom are women. Given reasons for this growth and the types of jobs part-time workers perform, there seems to be strong evidence that they are emerging as a new form of secondary labour force.

7 UNION STRATEGIES AND INTER-UNION COMPETITION

The theme of this book is the management of labour within a changing product market context characterised by growing competition and pressure on profit margins but with scope for continuing market growth. This chapter considers the response of the banking unions to this environment, and in so doing emphasises the importance of the long-standing insitutional competition between BIFU and the staff unions in the CBU. It demonstrates how their policies have been influenced by this rivalry, although certain areas of similarity between the unions are also noted, and explained in terms of the demands of their common constituents, the banks' staff. The organisational strategies of the unions are linked to efforts to resolve the inter-union rivalry by a merger, and the chapter explains why these efforts failed in terms of the continuing ideological differences between the two sides for, in turn, these differences have created deeply conflicting views over the appropriate distribution of power. Furthermore, it is suggested that in response to the less accommodating objectives of management a clearer differentiation in policies has emerged, reducing the common ground between the two sides. In effect, therefore, the influence of the employers is consistently stressed as a factor which has moulded the nature and outcome of the inter-union conflict.

Nature of the Rivalry

It is the origins and dimensions of this rivalry which are reconsidered first. These were discussed in Chapter 2 when the history of collective representation up to the end of the 1960s was traced. It was stressed that employer discrimination had a profound effect on the pattern of representation in the banks, influencing the nature and dimensions of competition between the staff bodies. This discrimination reflected the paternalistic employment policies of the banks which emphasised a common set of interests and discouraged external sources of loyalty. This conflicted with the philosophy of the national union which pursued the organisation of all bank staff regardless of their employer.

Out of this discrimination the ideological and organisational components of the inter-union rivalry were crystallised. The trade union's national orientation and objective of all-grades representation throughout the English banks derived from certain structural developments in the industry which affected all categories of staff around the time of its formation; furthermore, its geographical structure was a means of bridging the interests of clerks working in what were at the time regional banks, such as Martins, based around South Lancashire, and the Westminster Bank, in the home counties and London. In contrast, the associations reflected the strong enterprise-based nature of the banks' employment policies and the distinctiveness of banking as a career to suggest trans-enterprise linkages were of little relevance, and that the assumptions of more 'orthodox' trade unionism (dominated numerically by manual unions) were also inappropriate.

The preferential treatment by the banks towards the associations sharpened these distinctions. Initially, relations between the representative bodies were not axiomatically hostile, but the experience of discrimination led the union to regard the associations as illegitimate forms of staff representation obstructing real trade union organisation. In turn the associations' position also hardened. Each developed organisational principles and bargaining objectives designed to counterpose those of their rivals, and again the actions of the employers were influential. Immediately after the war NUBE had favoured a two-tier bargaining model, for example, but after formal enterprise-level rights were given exclusively to the associations in the 1950s the union became exclusively committed to national bargaining. In effect, it became a competition between *internalist* principles of the associations and the *externalist* principles of the national union. A further dimension of this rivalry was expressed in the policies concerning representative officers: although started by bank clerks, the national union began to employ its own full-time officials in the inter-war years in reaction to the associations' practice of relying entirely on lay-members who remained, until the 1970s, the full-time employees of their banks.

The rivalry also had an ideological dimension. The associations adhered to a co-operative philosophy, called 'internalism' (a term which was used disparagingly by their opponents) in which there was 'an emphasis upon the common interest of employer and employed' and, as the Midland Bank Staff Association stated in evidence to the Donovan Commission, 'The foundation of [the association's] existence is a joint furthering of the interests of the Bank and the Staff who are equally dependent upon one another for their well-being' (MBSA, 1965).

By focusing on the areas of common interest in the employment relationship the internalists claimed to be distinctive 'trade unions', but internalism was not a highly abstract or fixed doctrine, and the associations have adapted from being transparently passive management adjuncts to independent bodies which are formally certificated as trade unions. Internalism is a reflection of a set of loose working principles, but one which the associations insist still informs their activities. A CBU policy document, for instance, simply stressed that although it uses the same methods as other trade unions — 'consultation, participation and negotiation . . .' it seeks through force of argument to achieve its demands recognising that compromise not outright victory is the hallmark of that process' (CBU, 1980, p.1). Others have argued that the more co-operative approach does have an impact on bargaining outcomes, and is not simply a matter of 'style' (cf. Crompton and Jones, 1984; Swabe and Price, 1984). Perhaps most importantly this means the associations have generally opposed the use of sanctions, only recently adopting tightly limited strike clauses in their rules, mainly in response to statutory pressures. Speaking in 1972, for example, one association's general secretary emphasised:

> Both employer and employee derive their welfare from the same business, and sooner or later, both sides have to learn to live together in peace. This lends itself to the quiet working out of problems between Management and Staff, and appeals therefore to the thoughtful rather than to the militant. (MBSA General Secretary)

Secondly, they continue to denounce broader affiliations with the wider trade union movement such as through the TUC, although at times they have joined political pressure groups when this was thought appropriate. This again reflects the pragmatic element of the association's ethos.

Despite the longstanding criticism that they are employer dominated the survival and growth of the associations cannot be seen simply in terms of the approbation they received from the banks. Their success has also reflected the ability to transform themselves sufficiently to defend the monetary interests of their members while maintaining a distinctive image or character. Ideological expressions of co-operation with management may have found greater sympathy with their white-collar constituents, but the ability to complement this as effective bargaining agents was also crucial, for as Roberts *et al.* noted in their study of white collar unionists (1972) status concerns and monetary concerns were deeply inter-related. In effect, then, the associations have become very much like trade unions in the way they function, scoring highly on measures of organisational independence and bargaining demands — or what Prandy *et al.* (1982) call enterprise unionateness and the principal factor stimulating this transformation has been the competition from NUBE/BIFU.

The crucial measure of this competition has been membership and one measure of the success of the transformation of the staff associations into more 'unionate' bodies is shown by the continuing membership predominance of each staff union, as Figure 7.1 demonstrates. It also shows that from 1970 onwards the assumption which had carried the national union into joint working at the end of the 1960s was erroneous: the rapid growth in membership achieved prior to recognition was not sustained. Indeed, such was NUBE's loss of members between 1973 and 1976 that, although the Midland association transferred to ASTMS and thereby lost its national seat in 1974 and the Williams and Glyn's association transferred to NUBE in the same year, the associations had by then achieved such a rate of growth that they were able to recover from these setbacks within two years. NUBE's problems at this time are further underlined by the fact that clearing bank employment rose by 30,000 in the period 1969–78. Its density thus fell from 35.3 per cent at the beginning of this period to a low of 27.8 per cent at the end of 1975, before recovering marginally. The associations in contrast sustained a roughly stable density over the whole period, starting with around 40.5 per cent and finishing the period marginally higher (41.7 per cent).

Merger and Diversification

This failure by NUBE prompted two other strategies which were to have marked effects upon the conduct of labour relations in banking. First, the union began to diversify. Until 1970 the union had not spread much beyond the English and Scottish clearing banks, the Trustee Savings Bank, where it achieved pay-bargaining rights in the early 1960s, and certain international banks in which, in some cases, the clearing banks had a stake. In effect, it acknowledged the market and ownership divisions within the finance sector as setting the limits to its own territory. After 1970, financial pressures began to develop: inflation affected its expenditure, particularly its staffing costs and this problem was aggravated by the traditional reluctance to devolve responsibility to lay activists. The union felt particularly constrained by the lower subscriptions charged by the associations and as a result did not raise its subscriptions in line with costs in the late 1960s and first half of the 1970s

Figure 7.1: Union Membership: London Clearing Banks, 1970–84

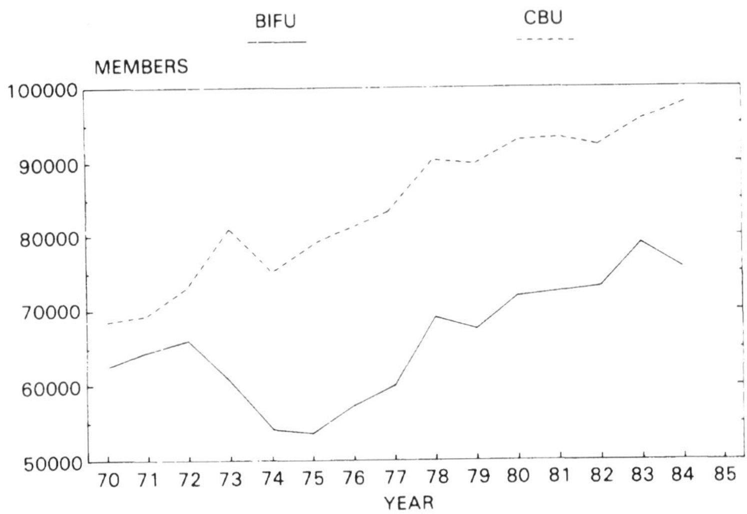

Source: Unions Records

(Willman and Morris 1985; Undy *et al.* 1981). As Latta (1972) has shown, NUBE was one of the least financially secure unions in existence, with minimal assets and expenditure regularly exceeding income. Partly to resolve this, motions proposing diversification into building societies and insurance were passed at the 1971 annual delegate meeting, but the executive was initially reluctant to pursue such growth, seeing it as non-cost effective without recognition.

The situation was changed by the Industrial Relations Act (1971). NUBE held out high hopes for this legislation, primarily as a means of having the associations outlawed, in a way which reflected its earlier reliance upon the Industrial Orders (1305 and 1376). Again, however, it was unsuccessful, not least, according to Dickens (1975), because the criteria for registration under the act were narrowly focused around financial independence. Each of the associations in the big four banks was able to register and as a result NUBE, too, felt obliged to register, if only to be protected against the threat of losing its recognition. Having done this in defiance of TUC policy NUBE was suspended, then expelled from the TUC in 1973, and exposed to competition from TUC unions such as ASTMS and APEX. The transfer of the MBSA to ASTMS in 1974 was the first fruit of this campaign. A second reason for registering was the expansion opportunities presented by use of Section 45 of the act in initiating applications for sole bargaining recognition or establishing agency shops. They presented a relatively cheap means of growth and one which potentially enabled the union to overcome employer hostility and staff association rivalry (NUBE, 1973).

More references were made by NUBE than any other union under the Act's provision (Weekes *et al.*, 1975). It achieved agency shop arrangements in the TSB, the Co-operative and Yorkshire Banks and it pursued recognition in building societies, where its success was confined to the smaller ones, in international banks, hire purchase companies and insurance. As a result, it became much less of a clearing bank based union in membership terms: in 1970, 77 per cent of its members were drawn from the London clearers; five years later the figure was nearly 20 per cent lower (58 per cent); by 1980 only half its members (51 per cent) were thus employed (Willman and Morris, 1985) and the union had formally signalled its wider organising ambitions by its name change in 1979 to the Banking, Insurance and Finance Union.

As a strategy, diversification did resolve certain problems facing the union: it managed, for example, to overcome its deep financial difficulties by by-passing the strong competition for membership growth it found in its original territory. However, it did not resolve the 'problem' of the associations, and this was tackled instead by proposals to merge. In fact discussions between the associations and the union coincided with NUBE's decision to diversify and have been almost continuous since the early 1970s, although three formal rounds can be identified. These are discussed in turn.

Association of Banking and Finance Unions

These talks were essentially a defensive move against the threatened incursion by ASTMS following its take-over of the Midland staff association. They started in September 1973, although for nearly two years before that NUBE had been pressing for discussion as a result of its falling membership and recognition that its strategy to dominate the associations through joint working was failing. The national union had also pressed the banks to influence the associations, and threatened to abandon joint working; it was taken seriously by the Federation directorate whose objective was relatively close to the prevailing orthodoxy of creating strong unified bargaining agents, preferably of TUC unions (see, for example, CIR Annual Reports; Strinati, 1982), but resisted by the majority of the banks' personnel managers, whose thinking displayed the more traditional concern to preserve the distinctive character of the associations which was threatened potentially by a merger. Their position only changed with the announcement of the MSBA executive of its recommendation of a transfer to ASTMS in September 1973. The prospect of dealing with a more aggressive TUC union, which announced a general recruiting campaign in the clearers following the transfer of the Midland Association, prompted the banks to press the associations into action with the promise of sole bargaining rights for the merged body. Talks commenced quickly under the chairmanship of a personnel executive from one of the banks.

Within four months a proposed structure for the new body had been outlined and a name agreed — the Association of Banking and Finance Unions. In the summer of 1974 the banks and staff bodies were confident of a rapid resolution to differences. However matters became bogged down when discussions over the relationships between different levels within the new body started and lay officials from each side were brought in to the process. It became clear that while the staff association activists saw any merged body as essentially a confederation of enterprise-level bodies with little authority or resources above that level, NUBE's lay members envisaged a strongly centralised union.

In particular, disagreement emerged on three issues: control of subscriptions, employment of officials and the level of membership. The associations preferred power and membership to be decentralised to the constituent parts which would be analogous to the existing staff associations, while NUBE envisaged power residing above the enterprise level units, not least to ensure ABFU was little more than a series of loosely linked 'internalist' associations. Other ideological differences also emerged over a proposed strike clause and the desirability of TUC affiliation, effectively stalling the talks by the spring of 1975, although meetings continued to take place until early 1976.

The underlying reasons for the initiative also became less urgent. First, NUBE began to arrest its membership decline in the clearing banks and to see the fruits of its diversification elsewhere. Its financial difficulties were also eased by signing several check-off arrangements as a result of its use of the Industrial Relations Act. These check-off arrangements also improved its cash flow by allowing the move to monthly direct debiting of subscriptions. The need for a merger inevitably involving a compromise of principles thus also became less attractive. Secondly, the threat of ASTMS never materialised; it was refused or declined national recognition and failed to spread to other banks. By 1975 its membership in the Midland was clearly not accelerating, as managers had feared, and its request for domestic pay bargaining was declined. Moreover, following the repeal of the Industrial Relations Act, NUBE successfully applied for re-entry to the TUC, thereby regaining some protection from inter-union competition under the Bridlington Rules but increasing the disagreement with the associations.

Yet the fundamental reason for NUBE to initiate the merger discussions had not been resolved. As the minority body it was still subject to control by the associations in negotiations and while still formally participating in the AFBU discussions it attempted to have them debarred from recognition by opposing their applications for certificates of independence under the new Labour government's legislation — unsuccessfully. The union was thrown back on its old strategy of pursuing majority membership and to do this it had to be able to demonstrate its greater effectiveness. It therefore resolved to withdraw from joint working, and was offered a suitable pretext when the associations insisted on putting forward a pay claim in the summer of 1977 which contravened the then operative phase (II) of the incomes policy. NUBE, as a TUC affiliate, argued that it had to support this and opposed the associations' claim. The irony of this was that NUBE broke off joint working with the associations, which it had long criticised as too moderate, ostensibly because it could not tolerate their attempt to break the pay policy.

The Johnston Enquiry

The second formal round of merger talks evolved directly from the collapse of joint working. NUBE immediately claimed separate bargaining rights, but the response of the banks revealed a complex set of factors at work. In some cases managers saw this as an opportunity to sever the links with NUBE and return to dealing exclusively with the associations; indeed NUBE was warned at the time that it would not be re-offered recognition if it withdrew. Others saw the opportunity to return to domestic bargaining either to obtain greater flexibility in the pay structure or, in Midland's case, to deal with ASTMS more effectively. However, in the short term dealing with the CBS alone put the Midland and Williams and Glyn's (where no association existed) in difficult positions, and to resolve this the Federation supported NUBE's proposal to bring in an outside party to resolve the division.

This party was Dr Tom Johnston, of Heriott Watt University. He was known as an experienced arbitrator who had demonstrated an interest in efficient centralised bargaining systems and his terms of reference were pitched broadly enough to encompass the question of reforming the bargaining structure, being 'to investigate the whole question of staff representation and negotiating procedures in the major London clearing banks, and to report with recommendations'. Johnston produced two reports (which he called Mark 1 and Mark 2) before these talks collapsed at the beginning of 1980.

Arguably, Johnston got much closer to securing a merger than the ABFU talks had. He built on the progress made in the former talks over the proposed structure of the merged body, in developing a three-tier model (Figure 7.2). But he also recognised that the ABFU talks had not been able to define the relationships between these levels, and particularly tried to resolve the outstanding problems of subscriptions, employment of officials and the point at which membership was held.

Figure 7.2: Johnston Report: Proposed Structure of Merged Union

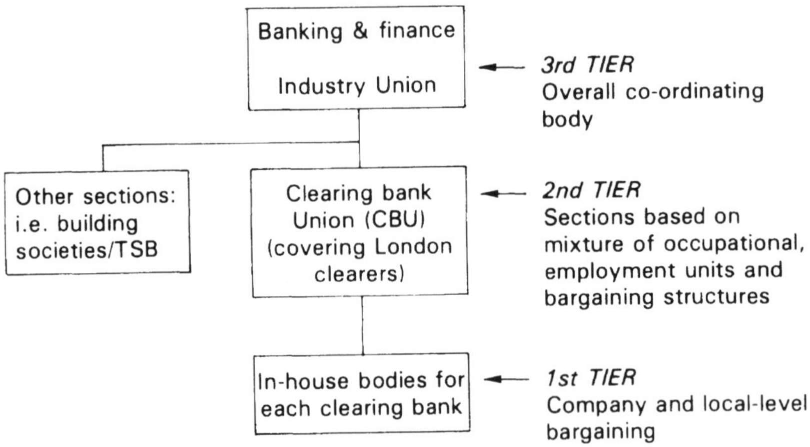

Source: Johnston (1978)

This was done both through written proposals and a sequence of meetings with the staff bodies at which Johnston adopted a conciliator role, thereby achieving a sequence of compromises both over the issues of organisational power, and over more ideological issues such as affiliation to the TUC (which was proposed and accepted). However, talks abruptly broke down late in 1979, ostensibly because BIFU would not accept Johnston's proposal that it return to joint working with the associations prior to merger as a gesture of good faith. Clearly, levels of trust between the two sides were still low, despite the compromises.

Underlying this, though, it seems that some lay groups were specifically concerned about the old problem of branch structure. On this point Johnston had explicitly rejected BIFU's request for geographically based branches, and this provoked concern that an internalist breakaway might be possible. Without the guarantee of a trans-institutional structure, the BIFU's executive could not recommend a merger, proposing instead further talks under heads of agreement defined by Johnston's reports. In this atmosphere the enquiry collapsed, with Johnston placing the blame squarely on BIFU in his postscript (Johnston, 1980).

But a further reason why Johnston's proposals petered out was that, again, the motivation to merge declined as the enquiry proceeded. Although the banks had threatened to withold recognition from BIFU, in practice they found it impossible to ignore the union. The context of this was the collapse of the incomes policy at the end of 1978 and a wages explosion throughout the economy following the entry of the Conservative Party to office in 1979. Without a formal bargaining procedure or a co-ordinated pay strategy, the banks found themselves susceptible to a series of leapfrogging claims at the enterprise level backed by threats of industrial action from BIFU, and to a lesser extent some of the associations. The first settlement that year was tentatively agreed at around 12 per cent; by the autumn it had risen to 16–18 per cent according to grade, backdated to 1 July. Disagreement between the banks over policy priorites emerged: some saw the reconstruction of stable relations with both unions through formal procedures at the enterprise level as crucial; others considered this unwise given that prior to any merger separate bargaining would be the only option, and that would be intrinsically unstable. None the less, by 1980 a mixture of formal and informal separate bargaining arrangements had been constructed. BIFU's demand for separate bargaining had effectively been conceded nationally and domestically, and Johnston thus found himself trying to bring the two sides together in a context of inter-union competition within the bargaining process.

Post-Johnston Discussions

Notwithstanding this breakdown, merger discussions have taken place again. The reasons for this relate first to the costs (of separate bargaining) and second, the failure of separate bargaining to bring about a swift resolution to the dualism. Some of these costs are financial, as both organisations are required to divert some resources into competing with their rival, and there is also a duplication of resources in recruiting, research, negotiation and administration.

More broadly, though, the cost of division has been exploited by the banks to push through their own objectives. For example, each of the banks has been able to reinstitute Saturday opening without negotiation with the staff bodies, and efforts to resist or regulate this jointly have been unsuccessful. Nor has either union been able to impose any control over the direction of decision-making on new technology, although both are aware of its potential implications for careers and staff numbers. It has also proved easy for the banks to divide the unions in pay negotiations and undermine opposition by settling with one side or the other since 1981 when the employers re-established their combined position in the Federation.

A second reason is that the membership stalemate continues. Membership is important not just because of the traditional question of control in any joint working or financial stability, but also because it is the perception of union officials that a key obstacle to raising the overall density level is the inter-union conflict. The prospect of recruiting the unorganised 30 per cent of bank staff is thus an incentive for both sets of union officials to pursue merger talks. In membership terms, BIFU remains a long way, in aggregate, behind the staff unions (now divisions of the Clearing Bank Union, CBU) and although its membership rose at a faster *rate* than the CBU's from the collapse of joint working to the end of 1984, in absolute terms BIFU has performed worse. It also faces further problems in due course, first owing to the departure of Williams and Glyn's from the Federation of London Clearing Bank Employers (where it had sole rights) in 1985, and secondly, with the integration of Barclays Bank International (where it had sole rights) and Barclays domestic division. The Barclays staff union (BGSU) can thus recruit in a new territory, and given its exceptional performance in the past, it is likely that BIFU will lose several thousand members in this former stronghold. But membership has not just been a problem for BIFU: not withstanding the BGSU's success, its co-divisions in Lloyds and National Westminster have seen their membership stagnate over the last seven years while BIFU's has risen (see Table 7.1).

It was these organisational matters which prompted the two sides to reopen talks. Merger discussions got under way in 1982 and formal meetings were held until the initiative collapsed in the autumn of 1985. Significantly, no outside party was invited to chair the discussions and there was also no attempt to build upon past progress; all was again open to negotiation. This raised the risk that without external direction the talks could easily become bogged down as in the past over the key issues affecting the distribution of organisational power or 'ideological' issues such as TUC affiliation and the calling of strikes. To get round this, working parties were set up to explore proposals on subscriptions, financing of the different levels and membership, but little agreement was reached. Furthermore, the old problem of the appropriate branch structure returned, and was unresolved when the CBU Annual Conference voted to withdraw from the discussions on fears that the Lloyds staff union would secede. Within the latter body, the powerful managers'

Table 7.1: Membership NUBE/BIFU — Staff Associations/Unions by Bank

Year	Barclays BIFU	SA	Lloyds BIFU	SA	Natwest BIFU	SA	Midland BIFU	SA	Wills/Glyn's BIFU	SA
1971	24,971	18,925	10,308	16,023	19,567	23,679	10,192	10,486	2,866	595[2]
1972	24,826	22,612	10,854	16,902	20,502	23,802	10,159	10,087	3,222	
1973	23,417	29,433	9,640	17,317	16,703	24,510	10,381	10,157[1]	3,801	
1974	20,024	31,898	9,247	17,921	13,999	25,708	9,717		4,044	
1975	18,301	31,966	10,537	19,403	13,328	27,770	10,328		3,814	
1976	18,797	31,920	11,658	20,563	14,156	29,270	11,542		4,201	
1977	18,638	32,788	12,786	21,306	14,090	29,990	13,031		4,580	
1978	18,556	35,517	15,257	21,247	13,887	33,556	16,520		4,962	
1979	16,061	35,788	15,558	20,913	14,421	33,269	17,079		4,485	
1980	15,381	38,846	16,088	21,004	16,080	32,969	19,828		4,650	
1981	14,874	39,228	15,985	20,227	16,332	33,718	20,546		4,874	
1982	14,176	39,400	16,057	20,436	16,857	32,552	20,825		5,215	
1983	15,418	41,200	17,661	21,000	18,739	33,750	21,722		5,484	
1984	14,312	42,099	16,150	21,268	17,864	34,300	21,776		5,603[3]	
1985	15,346	45,002	13,340	21,685	17,391	34,175	21,239			

Source: Unions' Records. NB: Basis of calculation changed in 1978

Notes: 1 Thereafter ASTMS; figures not available

2 WGSA transferred to NUBE

3 From Sept. 1985 Williams and Glyn's no longer exists independently

committee was particularly opposed to merger talks, not least because the staff union has sole representative rights for managerial grades in Lloyds. More generally it seems that lay activists from each of the interested parties were more sceptical about the need for co-operation than the full-time officials and placed a brake upon the talks as with the ABFU discussions. There is, then, still considerable distance between the two sides.

Furthermore, as BIFU diversifies more, it arguably increases the barriers. Only 48 per cent of its members are now in the London clearers and although they still dominate the national executive, a majority of members are unconcerned directly with the outcome. Diversification may be seen as a more attractive alternative to merger if it does not involve compromising principles (Buchanan, 1981) but it may also make it more difficult to devise an organisational structure acceptable to the incoming associations which would always wish to maximise their autonomy.

Areas of Consensus

Paradoxically, however, despite the failures to achieve a merger there are grounds for seeing similarity in the strategies of the two competing unions in the past. This has stemmed from their common constituency, with each perceiving the need to reflect the moderate image of bank clerks. For the staff bodies engaged in an institutional competition, this has posed certain tensions between the need to be effective and the need to avoid militancy.

The clearest example of how this ambiguity could operate has been shown in the issue of conflict resolution. For the national union, the need to support arbitration provisions stemmed from the view that bank workers, as the 'aristocracy of clerks' (Lockwood, 1958; Allen and Williams, 1960), were unlikely to support direct action. Making a virtue of a necessity the union thus proclaimed its preference for such 'reasonable' and sensible methods of conflict resolution while at the same time it insisted on having a strike clause to demonstrate its commitment to the principles of independent trade unionism, and to contrast itself to the associations. In fact only after a rule change in 1960 was it really possible for the union to organise a strike and even then, in keeping with the centralised nature of the organisation, only the national executive could authorise this. Subsequently recognition created the dilemma of whether to rely on arbitration or on the direct enforcement of claims by sanctions; NUBE, despite the period of success in the 1960s in taking strike action in the TSB as well as the clearers in pursuit of recognition, opted for the safety of arbitration. In that sense, the union chose to compete with the associations by demonstrating it was as moderate and respectable but this, then, made it impossible for NUBE to compete on the grounds of greater effectiveness.

Conversely, for the staff associations the reliance upon arbitration did not conflict with their effectiveness, but underpinned it. Arbitration facilitated their transition from passive management adjuncts to bargaining agents while sustaining their 'distinctive' non-coercive character. When these facilities were withdrawn this threatened the grounds on which they competed with BIFU both by exposing the issue of their bargaining effectiveness and by challenging the premise of an underlying identity of interests between employers and employees on which internalism was based. It left the staff unions with little option but to become more unionate to sustain their claims to be effective representative agents and this indeed happened. For example, the BGSU executive recommended limited industrial action over the re-introduction of Saturday working in 1983 and in its pay negotiations in 1985. Each of the CBU divisions had also considered introducing less restrictive strike clauses, but thus far has not done so.

However, greater unionateness has been balanced by a continuing stress upon the other competitive factor, namely co-operation. This has been achieved by emphasising: one, a pragmatic problem-solving approach in contrast to the desire of other unions to 'milk' every issue; two, the superior knowledge of officials drawn from the banks' employment; supported by, three, extensive lay structures from the bank branch upwards which can 'react speedily [and] get to the root of problems' (quote, General Secretary BGSU).

The similarity in policies associated with the competition for members is further influenced by the vertical integration of both unions. All-grades representation mutes the tendency for competition to be developed through the pursuit of sectional interests: instead, both the union and staff associations have behaved as what Olson has termed 'encompassing organisations' (Olson, 1976) in so far as they have both usually sought to distribute advantages evenly throughout the different grades and across the clearing bank sector. In the past, this offset the pursuit of competitive advantage through bargaining. Most clearly this was demonstrated in the pay-bargaining policies of each side which, throughout the 1970s, were principally directed to maintaining stable differentials against the compressive effects of employers trying to limit wage costs and periods of incomes policy. This similarity is in some senses surprising given the difference in profiles of membership for this might have been expected to provoke greater sectionalism. The associations have long claimed a higher proportion of senior (i.e. career) staff, while BIFU is more strongly represented in the lower grades: in 1983, 12 per cent of LBGSU members were in managerial grades and approximately 3 per cent of BIFU's Lloyds members were. It might therefore have been expected that BIFU would develop policies which favoured the majority of its members, by pressing for a narrowing of differentials in terms and conditions, as the basis of its competitive differentiation from the associations.

This did not occur because each union's policies were deliberately designed to equalise its appeal across the whole range of bank staff as the means of maximising its growth potential. However, there was another reason for the policy similarities. Like the associations, NUBE/BIFU was also committed to the notion of banking as a career long after this had become inaccurate for the majority of staff. It therefore supported the principle of a progressive pay structure as the crucial element of an equitable salary strategy. A NUBE pamphlet published in 1978 stressed the need for greater attention to the distortion (i.e. compression) of differentials caused by pay policies and called for a system based on 'real ability' to create an 'ordered' and 'rational' structure. More predictably, at the same time staff association propaganda called for the reopening of differentials to reward managerial responsibility adequately. In sum, mediating the institutional competition and different membership base was an area of consensus between the key policies of the union and associations which derived from the assumption of banking as a career and bank staff as normatively committed to a career-based reward structure.

The Emergence of Policy Differentiation

But in the recent context of the more intensive inter-union rivalry and the changes in the banks' labour relations policies prompted by the evolving product market conditions, the policy consensus has broken up. On pay, BIFU has made a sequence of claims designed to narrow differentials between the junior clerical grades and other staff. To an extent this is evidently explicable by reference to the union's membership profile; but this change reflects a more pessimistic set of assumptions about employment and career prospects which is seen to require a broader challenge to management control. The harder line management policies has thus also contributed to the greater policy differentiation between the unions.

Central to this is the introduction of new technology. In the last chapter it was shown that technical innovations have a direct bearing on the nature of competition and the organisation of work in banking, and BIFU now sees these as a threat to jobs, career opportunities and skills (BIFU, 1982). Breaking from past policies, which were predicated upon acceptance of managerial control over all but the limited area of pay and conditions of work, it has sought to extend the area of joint determination to include the planning, design and installation of new equipment. This implies the negotiation of manning levels, working practices and job content, training, career development and promotion criteria. Another novel aspect of BIFU's policies can be discerned in its claim for a sharing of the benefits of rising productivity by proposing a 28 hour, 4 day week, increased holidays and a voluntary retirement age of 55. This is also designed to sustain employment levels in banking. It represents a fundamental departure from the traditional means by which the benefits of technical innovation have been allocated in banking, however such a degree of joint regulation is also quite out of step with the tradition of high managerial control in the finance sector. Although BIFU has achieved consultative rights in the Co-operative Bank, and in the TSB secured no-redundancy guarantees as well as reductions in working hours in certain pilot agreements, in the clearers its success has been very limited. None of them will sign its new technology model agreement, or accept the principles therein as negotiable, despite being willing to bargain about certain aspects of working the new equipment.

Linked to this is concern over the prospects for non-career staff, particularly women. BIFU has argued recently that women will increasingly occupy routine clerical jobs with little opportunity for promotion, and have to bear the brunt of 'de-skilling' occuring through automation. It has therefore called for 'positive action programmes' for women, more training and retraining to enhance promotion prospects, reduced hours and more rapid movement through grade scales (BIFU, 1985). Again, however, it has had little success in negotiating such changes. This is not to conclude that BIFU is intrinsically opposed to technical change, rather it is pursuing what Slichter *et al.* (1960) termed an adjustment strategy to influence the terms under which it occurs by, for example, restricting counter-terminals to bank offices, and obtaining exclusive control over certain jobs — such as refilling cash machines — regardless of whether they are placed in a bank or a supermarket.

Although the same may broadly be said of the CBU, its policies do differ from BIFU's. In their policy document on new technology, the staff unions have proposed consultation over its introduction with no compulsory reductions in management posts created by the segmentation of branch networks in Barclays and National Westminster. Yet such changes have served to heighten the dilemma facing the associations which on one hand wish to act as a trade union in defending members interests while, on the other, endorsing managerial objectives in pursuing efficiency as being in the best long-term interests of their members. Explicitly, the staff unions have reaffirmed their support for management's right to manage (CBU, 1985) and beyond consultation over the *in situ* problems of installing new equipment make no claims for greater control. This is because underlying their thinking there remains a greater optimism for the future growth prospects of the industry and, thus, employment levels, so no justification for extended control over work organisation is assumed to exist. Instead, the CBU's policies seek to influence the immediate costs of change to affected groups whilst supporting, in principle, managerial objectives in determining technical change and appropriate organisational forms. The 'adjustment' is premised on different terms.

Yet in terms of the inter-union competition, the effects of this greater policy differentiation have not been dramatic. In particular, there has not been a reversal in the relative strengths of membership, which has always been the key competitive indicator. While BIFU hopes to take advantage of slower employment growth and declining career prospects to raise its membership through what Bain and Eisheikh have called the 'threat' effect (1976) it faces a number of problems. In particular, as Crompton and Jones (1984) have shown, female workers (who constitute the majority of unorganised bank staff) may not be predisposed to take up union membership as a result of 'de-skilling' or reduced job prospects. Other strong structural influences, including the branch pattern of membership and the influence of local managers on membership selection, may mediate BIFU's efforts to grow by concentrating on junior staff (Blackburn, 1967; Riseborough, 1982). Meanwhile, such policy differentiation is only likely to make more difficult the resolution of the inter-union competition through merger.

Conclusions

This chapter has considered the changing nature of the relationship between the unions in the clearing banks. It argued that the long-standing and unique form of rivalry between them was fundamental to understanding their organisational behaviour and objectives. This institutional competition was, in turn, influenced by the banks' labour strategies and by the common perception that the unions' constituents — bank staff — were by and large of a moderate disposition and exceptionally committed to sharing the goals of their employers.

Historically, the unique form of inter-union rivalry evolved because of employer discrimination in favour of the staff associations. The national union has, in consequence, always regarded the association as employer dominated to a certain extent, and an obstacle to true trade union representation. Over the past 40 years it has made repeated but unsuccessful attempts to have the associations debarred from recognition through reference to various government statutes.

The associations' success in surviving as bargaining agents under the pressure of BIFU's competition was related to their continuing ability to attract members. In turn this was explained by their success in transforming themselves from passive, powerless bodies into independent representatives functioning like trade unions while sustaining their distinctive ethos. While there was ostensible co-operation through joint working for ten years from 1968–78, the underlying rivalry meant that BIFU consistently sought to overturn its subordinate position. One strategy was by merger, but talks towards this end have been undermined by the ideological differences between the unions. Hence, the national union has insisted on more direct competition through separate bargaining since 1978. This strategy reflects a long-standing assumption that membership preferences are largely determined by bargained outcomes which are in turn a result of union effectiveness. Thus far, however, even the demonstration of greater effectiveness has proved problematic, because the employers have been able to exploit the inter-union divisions and because BIFU has not been able to galvanise its (moderate) staff into action. The membership gap between the two sides remains in the associations' favour.

More recently a new dimension to the inter-union competiton has emerged in response to the less accommodating management policies of the banks. This concerns real differences in the objectives and priorities of the unions which in the past were largely absent; in effect while the CBU has continued to adopt a relatively economistic set of policies, with limited consultative rights in other areas, BIFU is now attempting to challenge management control over a much broader range of work issues, albeit with little success. This reflects a more pessimistic view of the future employment and career prospects in the industry and it has implications for the inter-union competition, suggesting that as their differences increase a merger becomes more problematic. Ironically, though, both BIFU and the staff unions recognise that their negotiating environment is becoming more hostile and that the continuing division has exposed their weaknesses: undermining the achievement of an effective representative voice at a time when this may, to their own members, be seen as increasingly important.

8 CONCLUSIONS AND PROSPECTS

The theme of this book has been the impact of changing business objectives upon the management of labour. At the outset it was argued that although recent work has recognised the importance of the former on the latter, there remain gaps in our understanding of how this relationship operated in practice. These relate to difficulties in analysing the nature of strategic decision-making as well as an inadequate understanding of the central business strategies in a dynamic context. For these reasons the book has adopted an approach which traced the links between the commercial decision-making context facing the banks and their employee relations policies over a time period of some 20 years. It was noted that although decisions concerning labour are contingent upon, and downstream from, the central mission of the company — the achievement of a satisfactory return on the assets through decisions about market position and growth — none the less the management of labour also represents an input into these key areas of policy as a constraint and as an opportunity.

In this book it has been argued that strategies are concerned both with certain broad goals and with the methods adopted to reach them. These goals go beyond the range of issues jointly determined by management and unions, and include preferred methods of recruiting and retaining labour; the process of management development; motivation; consultation and communications; productivity growth; and the determination of pay and conditions of work. Relations with unions and the scope and structure of negotiation are also of strategic importance. It was also argued that the preservation of certain values stressing the desirability of high-trust relations between employees and senior management to ensure co-operation and commitment to the enterprise's objective was an important part of the managerial strategy for labour. Yet the use of the term strategies has to be qualified. As a picture of reality, the normative model of planned organisational change being derived from corporate policies to determine future action did not always hold true. Frequently, change has been cautious and incremental and decision making has occurred without planning in a purposive manner. Furthermore, those specialists concerned with employee relations could not invariably claim that their goals or the components of their policies fitted together in a coherent or integrated manner. In some areas there is certainly a high degree of forward planning, such as manpower requirements and management development. In other areas external events or other management groups have been very influential. Additionally, although it has been shown that substantive changes have taken place, the banks have adopted a passive approach to employee relations to the extent that they have been prepared to work on the basis of consensus decision making without the enterprise, in the national forum. So if it is accepted that the banks have had strategies in employee relations it also has to be acknowledged that these were embedded, as it were, in long-term corporate decisions rather than explicitly worked out in the initial stages of management planning. This seems to be partly because of the structure of senior management in general management teams which have then inhibited the development of specialist based influence in some functions such as employee relations. Partly as well, the lack of strategic power must stem from the absence of conflict and the ability of the banks to institute change with little fear of obstruction. For these reasons it can hardly be concluded that the banks' commercial success results from a more strategic approach to the management of their labour.

This returns us to the question raised in the introduction regarding the extent to which the employee relations the banks adopted contributed to commercial success and to what extent the exercise of management choice mattered. It was pointed out that labour relations have usually been regarded as critical in terms of the relative failure of certain industries or firms. The history of the British motor industry, and more specifically the last domestically-owned car manufacturer — BL — exemplifies this (Marsden *et al.*, 1985) but outside crises of falling profits or periods of loss, employee relations factors may not be so critical. Commercially, the clearing banks had the considerable advantage of a virtual monopoly in the retail sector and were perhaps more fortunate than other areas of British commerce in the scope for growth in markets at home and abroad they were able to exploit. Furthermore, the monopoly ownership of the clearing system and extensive branch networks represented considerable competitive advantages, allowing them to tap the post-war increases in demand for consumer and producer credit. This volume expansion has compensated for the loss of money transmission profits and the failure to sustain market share for sterling and currency deposits. Enormous volume growth in foreign currency markets in London is also a factor from which the clearers have been able to profit.

This is not to imply that there were no difficulties associated with growth. To achieve profitable expansion has required the displacement of manually performed tasks by automated processes, at enormous capital cost, while falling margins were occurring from the increasing competition in private and corporate markets. This placed growing pressure on the banks' labour costs, particularly as their labour intensiveness had made expansion over the past 20 years of relatively high wage inflation very expensive. What labour relations factors therefore permitted the banks to overcome these contextual difficulties and how significant were they?

A number of these factors were identified. These were in some senses complementary. First, the banks were able to offer security of employment to their staff and the opportunity for career progression, even if in practice only a minority of recruits could expect to reach managerial rank. In turn, this reflected on the importance of staffing business expansion in the post-war period with a growing proportion of females who were mainly expected to quit bank work voluntarily in their twenties, and achieved only truncated career progression within the clerical grades. This allowed those who did stay with their banking employer to achieve much greater career advance, and permitted the banks to manage fluctuations in business volume without widespread redundancy.

Secondly, the banks never experienced the sorts of job controls exercised by work groups in part of British manufacturing industry. This reflected the more co-operative attitude of the white-collar workforce, the management emphasis upon job rotation in clerical tasks and generalist training, which limited task specialisation, and the practice of transferring staff between a number of branches mainly within a local area during their careers, often through promotion. Collectively, these factors tended to inhibit the development of customary job 'property' rights, that is the idea that a certain group of workers owned, or had the right to determine the content of specific tasks. In addition, there was no strong union organisation at the shopfloor/office level: the national union was highly centralised and for many years inhibited any autonomy in organisation or bargaining amongst lay activists; the staff associations, while better organised locally, were opposed to strategies which might represent a challenge to managerial prerogative, and thus also made no attempt to decentralise negotiations. Retaining control of work methods and manning levels was crucial in so far as it allowed the banks to cope with business expansion profitably by the unfettered introduction of technical innovations from the mid-1960s onwards.

Divided staff representation was a third factor. Indeed, the unions were not simply divided, they were ideologically opposed and engaged in an institutional struggle for dominance which prevented proper co-ordination of resources and policy. Behind the hostility was a history of employer discrimination in favour of the staff associations, which were originally encouraged as an obstacle to trade union growth. These associations mirrored the paternalistic values of the banks in stressing co-operation and, despite the transformation into independent bargaining agents, consistently deplored the use of sanctions or the rhetoric of a conflict of interests in the employment relationship. Their popularity must, to a certain extent, have reflected the success of the banks in sustaining their paternalistic ideology; it also meant that the more orthodox union BIFU was usually too weak to impose its position either before recognition, or even afterwards in the bargaining process.

On their own, of course, the existence of these factors does not explain the success of the banks either in being able to grow profitably or in managing their conditions for commercial success. But it is arguable that these factors facilitated a high degree of managerial control in the area of labour relations. The very existence of this control and trust both within and without institutional channels then provided the banks with the scope to respond to the problem of increasing competition in the product market.

The direction of the response in the past 15 years has been towards greater enterprise-level control in labour relations. In the 1960s a high degree of inter-bank co-operation was prevalent and this was a function of several factors. Principal among these was the tight state of the labour market coupled with the high demand for staff. This was, however, traditionally managed informally. Formalisation of this process was encouraged by growing pressure from the staff bodies, on the national union's part for recognition, and on the part of the staff associations by their increasingly aggressive behaviour in the pay-bargaining process.

Employer and inter-union co-operation resulted in the formal establishment at the national level of collective bargaining, yet the scope of negotiation was narrowly economic. This arrangement actually provided certain advantages to the employers which were subsequently crucial to the management of growth under increasingly competitive product market conditions. It guaranteed the co-ordination of pay, thereby limiting the potential for inter-bank competition of labour. It provided a means of constraining the increasingly aggressive trade union, NUBE, within procedures which avoided industrial action. Thirdly, it protected managerial prerogative on non-negotiable issues at the enterprise level.

The consequences of this agreement were that, although constrained marginally by the arbitration facility, the banks were still able to pursue greater efficiency in labour management. A major change in this respect was the reform of the salary structure. This signalled a shift from the former paternalistically-based reliance upon experience and loyalty by placing much greater emphasis on merit. Regular assessments were introduced with the objective of distinguishing more systematically between career and non-career staff. By raising the quality of the former group the aim was to improve commercial performance. Secondly, the separation between the national negotiating machinery and management of the enterprise meant banks could pursue greater control over working methods and performance outside the bargaining arena. This they did through more systematic task measurement and introduction of unilaterally established effort levels. Thirdly, output was raised, principally by automating many areas of the money transmission process. This allowed the banks to cope profitably with growing volumes of paper being put through the clearing systems. Importantly, technical change raised output per employee so much that it obviated the need for any wholesale effort intensification to achieve necessary efficiency targets. This resulted in a significant degree of continuity in work methods which coupled with continuing employment expansion and career opportunity meant that many elements of the paternalistic employment relationship were preserved despite the growing emphasis upon efficiency. It also meant that the opportunity or propensity for either union or associations to establish control over matters of work organisation or methods was limited.

Broadly then, the banks' policies created a clear distinction between pay and effort which was reinforced by the multiple bargaining levels and the question of effort levels was closely related to the introduction of technical change which was managed within the enterprise with the minimum of union involvement. Thus no linkage was made between trends in pay and productivity and the two moved quite independently, as Figure 8.1 shows. Here a simple measure of productivity is used, namely the number of payment transactions per employee, and the index of pay is taken from changes to the minimum level of Grade 3 pay but this is roughly consistent with patterns in other grades. The indices are thus only indicative of broad trends but they confirm how the banks were able to raise productivity virtually consistently and furthermore to avoid the establishment of any relationship between this upward trend and pay levels.

Accelerating product market competition from the end of the 1970s has since destabilised the management of labour relations. This changed market environment emerged from the conjuncture of legal/political and technological catalysts (Llewellyn, 1985) which among other things has

Figure 8.1: Indices of Productivity and Pay in the Banks, 1970-85

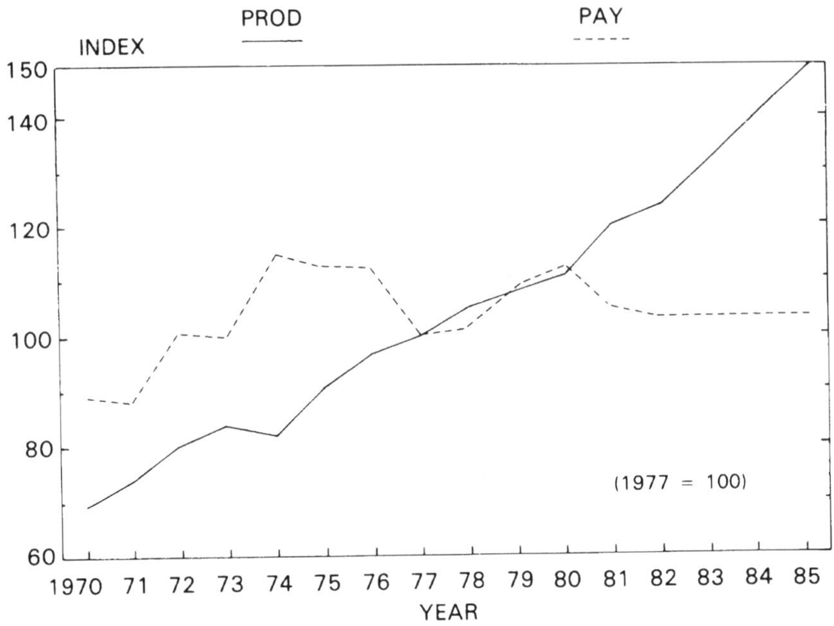

Source: CLCB

raised the prospect that the current *mode* of competition through the branch system is becoming extinct. Furthermore, just when the market environment had signalled the need for firmer control upon bargaining processes and outcomes another major threat to the former relative stability emerged. This was the eruption of inter-union competition and the collapse of joint working. In the area of joint negotiation this prompted changes to the procedures at national and company level. Notably, the compulsory arbitration facility, for long the guarantee of peaceful compromise, was not renewed despite the consequent risk of exposing the staff associations as impotent without resource to sanctions. Stability was sacrificed for stronger cost controls. If in consequence a greater *threat* of industrial action from both staff associations/unions and the national union resulted, and some small disputes actually occurred, this was the price of the employers relying upon their power to determine bargaining outcomes favourably, rather than accepting compromise solutions.

The substantive benefits of bargaining reform were demonstrated in several ways. First, a series of lower settlements were pushed through on the basis of a new set of bargaining criteria relating more closely to enterprise performance. Secondly, the scope of national negotiations was loosened as certain previously unresolved issues were reopened at the enterprise level. Thirdly, where issues were seen to be urgent the banks were able simply to ignore national agreements in implementing change, and in particular the reopening of branches on Saturdays. The banks pursued what one manager called '. . . a new desire to win on every issue' and in the bargaining process were able to exploit the weakness of union divisions, as all parties accepted. Hence, the conditions under which national bargaining had emerged as an employer strategy came into decline. Enterprise control over bargaining outcomes was accelerated by the restructuring of the industry and by an exceptionally deep profits crisis in one bank, the Midland, prompting its resignation from the Federation of London Clearing Bank Employers. Looser labour markets and falling demand for staff also reduced the need for employer co-ordination. Technical changes introduced the potential for greater task variety and organisational heterogeneity, and this is now placing a strain on the industry-wide grading system.

Consistent with the greater assertiveness in the bargaining process was the pursuit of increased efficiency in non-negotiable areas. In terms of working methods, more systematic control was established and job measurement either extended or recalculated. Evidence of effort intensification recently emerged in some banks. In the application of new technologies, branch restructuring became possible as efforts to link services more closely to market demand developed. For the first time, small numbers of staff were made redundant, and the banks began to indicate publicly that in future they could not guarantee full security of employment. To counter the potentially deteriorating effects on their paternalistic employment relationship, communications and consultation direct with staff as well as the unions were stepped up. Overall, the pursuit of increased efficiency has involved revisions both to the wage and the effort bargain, but to different extents within each bank; greater diversity has emerged in the content of enterprise-level strategies.

In general, it has been argued that the nature and degree of competitive pressure in the product market have been key influences upon management labour strategies over the past 25 years. Yet certain values have also been influential. Notions of a paternalistic employment relationship have entered decisions on relations with representative bodies in the way that conflict avoidance has been a high priority and in substantive issues such as the nature of the banks reward policies. Embedded in management thinking has been the belief in loyalty between employer and employees. This has not, however, acted as a constraint in the management of commercial change and paternalism has in some ways assisted the banks in lubricating the increasingly difficult adjustment process assisted by the weakness and division between the representative bodies. This division meant that both unions effectively concurred until recently in the distinction between pay and output which was crucial to cost effective expansion in such a labour-intensive business. For the national union this reflected its commitment to national bargaining and its mistaken assumption that recognition would be the precursor to majority membership and control of the associations. This meant that although formally recognised, it effectively had no power in the bargaining process for some ten years, to 1978. The associations, on the other hand, did pursue productivity-based pay claims prior to being drawn into national bargaining but then abandoned this criterion because it was thought inapplicable above the company level.

Throughout the last 25 years, the two sides have formed ideological differences which present too great an obstacle to securing a merger, despite this apparently being a necessary precondition for any degree of bargaining leverage. Their natural concern for institutional dominance might, in other circumstances, have been to the detriment of the employers if it had resulted in fragmented bargaining and 'leapfrogging'. As it stands, though, neither union has demonstrated the power to exploit the division to its own advantage or that of its members. This has been a somewhat fortuitous advantage for the banks at a time when they have seen it necessary to redraw the parameters of negotiation, and to initiate the profound organisational changes which are beginning to occur.

For the future, greater enterprise diversity in policies will be accompanied by certain common trends determined in a major way by technical change. Greater decentralisation of responsibilities for lending, growth and profits will be combined with increased centralised control and monitoring. Methods of assessing staff performance and the criteria involved are increasingly being directed towards branch performance. Associated with this are moves to link managerial rewards more closely to results, implying a wholesale reconstruction of the long-standing pay structure.

As the customer market becomes mature and competition intensifies as other companies (such as the TSB) enter the marketplace, the pursuit of indiscriminate growth is giving way to more differentiated business strategies. For example, all of the banks are seeking high net worth private customers and commercial business, but some may seek to reduce volume or specialise. In some respects this has already started to occur:

for instance, National Westminster specialises more in small businesses and markets itself to high net worth individuals through its separate subsidiary, Coutts and Co. Branch segmentation may well be accompanied by geographical restructuring based on population wealth and banks may once more become more regionally based.

The outcome is likely to be continued pressure for more heterogeneous labour policies, but certain common trends will also occur. Tasks will change as the banks pursue marketing more methodically: the beginnings of this can be seen in efforts to retrain 'tellers as sellers' and by pilot projects which have revised the layout of branches, introducing open-plan offices without security walls and enlarging the customer area at the expense of the back office. The general thrust of task changes and retraining will thus be towards the selling and sales administration of financial products rather than the processing of items through the clearing system. This is likely to influence reforms of the job evaluation system through which the banks will pursue the key strategic goal of flexibility in labour management. One possible change would be to reduce the number of grades and the large number of incremental steps in the career path in preference for a greater amount of task flexibility and less rigidly define jobs. This would be linked to a clearer distinction in tasks and training between a core group of future managerial stock and the remainder. Staff numbers will fall in the longer term: one senior Barclays manager predicted a drop of 5,000 in ten years in his bank (Long Range Planning, June 1985). Of these cuts most will fall on clerical and some supervisiory jobs, but a programme of massive redundancies is unlikely to occur given the sizeable 'secondary' labour force of female clerical staff whose turnover enables the banks to manage changing demand relatively flexibly.

As it has been argued that national co-ordination it best seen as a phase which is already in decline, one likely outcome is the reform of the employers' federation (the FLCBE). Already Williams and Glyn's has left following the operational unification with the Royal Bank of Scotland to become a UK bank. The Midland has also withdrawn and each fixes conditions of employment at the company level. The Federation may likewise become a UK body by combining with the Scottish Bankers' Federation — informal links have long existed and conditions of service are closely co-ordinated. In so doing it may adopt a looser advisory role similar to other employers' bodies.

Decentralising pay and performance measures also has implications for managerial control strategies. If each branch is more tightly appraised in terms of its contribution to overall performance, the notion of a paternalist employer providing the support of the wider corporate body is thereby less applicable. Two other factors are also relevant here; first, the declining number of career staff and the increasingly formal distinction between career and non-career employees, because to the latter group the loyalty, security and advancement implied in the paternalistic relationship have arguably never been so germane to their commitment to working for a bank. Secondly, according to Cowan (1982), there is an increasing likelihood of inter-bank recruitment associated with a greater degree of occupational specialisation to deal both with different types of product market and with the demand for data-processing skills. As the concept of a life-time career in one banks recedes, so does the paternalistic notion of a special framework of shared values and interdependence in the employment relationship.

Part of this policy involves the relations with trade unions. It was argued that in response to the growing competitiveness of banking the unions are also trying to formulate strategies. BIFU in particular has responded to the current and forthcoming changes in the industry by a radical shift in its policies over the last five years. How this dualism will be resolved in the future remains difficult to predict; despite the continual interest shown in a full merger by both the CBU and BIFU, the two sides appear to be becoming more differentiated in their policies and more entrenched ideologically (Morris, 1986). Nor has an organisational crisis such as a severe membership fall or loss of recognition occurred to prompt a more defensive alliance (Undy *et al.*, 1981). BIFU's diversification might suggest it is better placed to cope with changing product market boundaries, but its total density in the finance sector is low and in many areas it faces the old problem of hostile employers unwilling to deal with it, such as the building societies and many of the foreign banks (Willman and Morris, 1985). For the associations, the pragmatic balancing of co-operation and effectiveness, which has been at the heart of their ability to survive in the past, is increasingly difficult. In the longer term, an employment decline and reduced career opportunities may represent a threat to the old tenet of co-operation. A loss in actual and potential membership might also create organisational difficulties. The staff unions are relatively small, together having a membership of around 100,000, and although a relatively high proportion of their income derives form non-subscription sources they clearly experience certain diseconomies which might be resolved by merger (Buchanan, 1981).

Secondly, the staff unions are exposed to the charge that co-operation is increasingly tantamount to ineffectiveness because of the loss of arbitration rights. Already this has been raised by the banks' unilateral decision to reopen on Saturdays, regardless of the views of the staff bodies. Previously it was argued that the staff unions have responded by becoming more unionate, constitutionally at least. Their fundamental competitive problem concerns how much further they can pursue this line of change to remain effective without corroding their co-operative image which has long been the basis of differentiation from their rival in seeking membership growth. The danger from them remains that BIFU's membership has in the past risen relatively during periods of crisis in labour relations when the staff associations have seemed incapable of responding with sufficient strength. Previously the banks' response was more conciliatory at times of crisis; in the future this may not be the case and the associations then find themselves squeezed with less ground for co-operative solutions to exploit.

Continuing weakness may therefore be predicted and as the finance sector remains an area with considerable scope for unionisation, it is not unreasonable to assume that other unions may well enter the territory, altering the possibilities for competition and merger. As in the past, much will depend on the strategic decisions of the employers.

BIBLIOGRAPHY

Adams, R. (1975) 'Research Note: The Recognition of White Collar Workers Unions', *British Journal of Industrial Relations*, vol. 13, no. 1.

Allen, V. and S. Williams (1960) 'The Growth of Trade Unionism in Banking', *The Manchester School* (September), pp. 299–318.

Alexander, K.J. (ed.) (1975) *The Political Economy of Change* (OUP).

Bain, G.S. (1970) *The Growth of White Collar Trade Unionism* (OUP).

Bain, G.S. (ed.) (1983) *Industrial Relations in Britain* (Blackwell).

Bain, G.S. and F. Elsheikh (1976) *Union Growth and the Business Cycle* (Blackwell).

Banking Information Service (1981a) *The Banks and Small Firms*.

——— (1981b) *The Case against the Banking Levy*.

Banking Insurance and Finance Union (BIFU) (1980) *Report of the Microelectronics and Sub-committee*.

——— (1982) *Microtechnology: a Programme for Action*

——— (1983) *New Technology in Banking, Insurance and Finance*.

——— (1985) *Jobs for the Girls?*

Barnes, D. and E. Reid (1980) *Government and the Trade Unions: The British Experience, 1964–1979* (PSI).

Batstone, E., I. Boraston and S. Frenkel (1977) *Shop Stewards in Action* (Blackwell).

Batstone, E., A. Ferner and M. Terry (1984) *Consent and Efficiency* (Blackwell).

Batstone, E. (1984) *Working Order* (Blackwell).

Bevan, T. (1985) 'The Banking Environment', *Barclays Review*, vol.LX, no. 1.

Blackburn, R.M. (1967) *Union Character and Social Class* (Batsford).

Blackburn, R.M. and K. Prandy (1965) 'White-Collar Unionisation: a Conceptual Framework', *British Journal of Sociology*, vol. 16.

Boleat, M.J. (1980) 'Competition between Banks and Building Societies', *National Westminster, Quarterly Review* (November).

Buchanan, R. (1981) 'Mergers in British Trade Unions, 1949–79', *Industrial Relations Journal*, vol. 12, no.3.

Building Societies Association (1983) 'The Future Constitution and Powers of Building Societies' (January, unpublished).

B.S.A. (1984) 'New Legislation for Building Societies' (February, unpublished).

Certification Officer for Trade Unions and Employers' Associations (1979) *Staff Associations Supplement to the Annual Report* (HMSO).

Chalude, M. (1984) *Women and Job Segregation in Banking: The Status of Women their Roles, Change*, Report to the Commission of the European Community, Director M. Bolle de Bal.

Chandler, A. (1962) *Strategy and Structure* (Anchor: NY).

Child, D. (1984) *Payment Clearing Systems. Review of Organisation Membership and Control*, chairman D. Child (Banking Information Service).

Child, J. (1969) *British Management Thought* (George, Allen and Unwin)

——— (1985) 'Managerial Strategies: New Technology and the Labour Process' in D. Knights *et al.* (1985).

Child, J. and M. Tarbuck (1985) 'The Introduction of New Technology in Banking: Managerial Initiative and Union Response', *Industrial Relations Journal* (Autumn), vol.16, no.3.

Clearing Bank Union (1980) *Policy Statement*.

——— (1985) *New Technology and Developments*.

Clegg, H.A. (1976) *Trade Unionism under Collective Bargaining* (Blackwell).
——— (1979) *The Changing Sytem of Industrial Relations in Great Britain* (Blackwell).
Colwyn Committee Report (1918) *Report of a Treasury Committee on Bank Amalgamations,* Cmnd 9052.
Commission on Industrial Relations (CIR) (1973) *Williams and Glyn's Bank,* Report no. 34 (HMSO).
Committee of London Clearing Banks (CLCB) (1978) *The London Clearing Banks: Evidence by the CLCB to the Committee to Review the Functioning of Financial Institutions* (CLCB).
——— (1981) *The Case Against the Banking Levy.*
Counter Information Services (CIS) (1983) *Banking on the City,* Report no. 33.
Cowan, L.D. (1982) *Effects on Staff and Organisation in the Banks and Technology in the 1980s* (IOB).
——— (1985) 'The Impact of Technology in Banking' in Livy (ed.).
Crompton, R. (1976) 'Approaches to the Study of White Collar Trade Unionism', *Sociology,* vol. 10, no. 3.
Crompton, R. and G. Jones (1984) *White Collar Proletariat: Deskilling and Gender in Clerical Work* (Macmillan).
Davies, G. and J. Davies (1984) 'The Revolution in Monopoly Theory', *Lloyds Bank Review,* no. 153.
Deaton, D. and P. Beaumont (1980) 'The Determinants of Bargaining Structure: Some Large Scale Evidence for Britian', *British Journal of Industrial Relations,* XVIII, no. 2.
Dickens, L. (1975) 'Staff Associations and the Industrial Relations Act: the Effect on Union Growth', *Industrial Relations Journal,* vol. 6, no. 3.
Doeringer, P. and M. Piore (1971) *Internal Labour Markets and Manpower Analysis* (Lexington:Heath)
Donovan Report (1968) *The Report of the Royal Commission on Trade Unions and Employers' Associations,* Cmnd. 3523 (HMSO)
Dufty, N. (1978) 'Collective Bargaining in the Context of Compulsory Arbitration. The Case of the Western Australian Firemen', *British Journal of Industrial Relations,* vol. XVII, no. 3.
Dunkley, P. (1984) 'Base Rate: the Random Factor in Clearing Bank Productivity', *The Banker,* February.
Edwards, P.K. (1983) 'The Pattern of Collective Industrial Action', in G.S. Bain (ed.) (1983).
Edwards, R. (1979) *Contested Terrain: The Transformation of the Workplace in the Twentieth Century* (Heinemann).
Egan, A. (1982) 'Women in Banking: A Study in Inequality'. *Industrial Relations Journal,* vol. 13, no. 3.
Etzioni, A. (1961) *A Comparative Analysis of Complex Organisations* (Free Press).
Fels, A. (1972) *The British Prices and Incomes Board* (CUP).
Ferner, A. (1985) Political Constraints and Management Strategies: The Case of Working Practices in British Rail', *British Journal of Industrial Relations,* no. 1.
Flanders, A. (1975) *Management and Unions* (Faber).
Fox, A. (1966) *Industrial Sociology and Industrial Relations,* Research Paper 3, Donovan Commission (HMSO).
——— (1974) *Beyond Contract: Work Power and Trust Relations* (Faber).
Frazer, P. and D. Vittas (1982) *The Retail Banking Revolution* (Michael Lafferty)
Frazer, P. (1982) 'How Not to Measure Bank Productivity', *The Banker* (August)
Gaskin, M. (1974) *The Scottish Banks: a Modern Survey* (George, Allen and Unwin).
Gaskin, M. and B. Gaskin (1980) 'Employment in Insurance Banking and Finance', *ESU Research Papers,* no. 2.
Heritage, J. (1982) 'Feminisation and Unionisation: A Case Study from Banking' (University of Warwick, mimeo).

Hickson, D. and G. Mallory (1981) 'Scope for Choice in Strategic Decision Making and the Trade Union Role', in A. Thompson and M. Warner (eds.).

Hyman, R. and R. Price (eds.) (1983) *The New Working Class? White Collar Workers and Their Organisations* (Macmillan).

Inter-Bank Research Organisation (1982 & 1985) *Research Briefs: Consumer Payments and Financial Behaviour* (IBRO).

Institute of Directors (1984) *Settling Disputes Peacefully.*

Johnston, T.L. (1975) 'Arbitrating Industrial Change', in K.J.W. Alexander (ed.).

——— (1978/80) 'Reports of an Enquiry into Staff Representation in the Major London Clearing Banks' (unpublished).

Kahn-Freund, O. (1977) *Labour and the Law* (Stevens).

Kelly, J. (1984) 'Management Strategy and The Reform of Collective Bargaining: Cases from the British Steel Corporation', *British Journal of Industrial Relations*, vol. XXII, no. 2.

Kinnie, N. (1982) 'Local versus Centralised Bargaining: The Dangers of a "Halfway House"', *Personnel Management* (January).

——— (1985) 'Changing Management Strategies in Industrial Relations', *Industrial Relations Journal*, vol. 16, no. 4.

Kirchner, E., N. Hewlett and F. Sobirey (1984) *The Social Implications of Introducing New Technology in the Banking Sector*, Commission of the European Community, Luxembourg.

Knights, D. *et al.* (eds.) (1985) *Job Redesign: Critical Perspectives on the Labour Process*, (Gower).

Kochan, T., R. Mckersie and P. Cappelli (1984) 'Strategic Choice and Industrial Relations Theory', *Industrial Relations*, vol. 23, no. 1.

Latta, G. (1972) 'Trade Union Finance', *British Journal of Industrial Relations*, vol. X, no. 3.

Legge, K. (1978) *Power, Innovation and Problem Solving in Personnel Management* (McGraw-Hill).

Liddle, R. and W.E.J. McCarthy (1972) 'The Impact of the Prices and Incomes Board on the Reform of Collective Bargaining', *British Journal of Industrial Relations*, vol. X, no. 3.

Livy, B. (ed.) (1985) *Management and People in Banking*, 2nd edn. (IOB).

Llewllyn, D. (1985) 'The Changing Structure of the UK Financial System', *Three Banks Review*, no. 145.

Lockwood, D. (1958) *The Blackcoated Worker* (George, Allen and Unwin).

Marsden, D., T. Morris, P. Willman and S. Wood (1985) *The Car Industry. Labour Relations and Industrial Adjustment*, (Tavistock).

Marsden, D. (1982) 'Career Structures and Training in Internal Labour Markets in Britain and a Comparison with West Germany', *Manpower Studies*, 4 (IMS).

Marti, J. and A. Zeilinger (1982) *Micros and Money: New Technology in Banking and Shopping*, (PSI).

McCarthy, W.E.J. and N. Ellis (1973) *Management by Agreement: an Alternative to the Industrial Relations Act* (Hutchinson).

Megaw Report Inquiry into Civil Service Pay, Cmnd 8590 (HMSO).

Midland Bank Staff Association (1965) Evidence to the Donovan Commission.

Mintzberg, H. (1978) 'Patterns in Strategy Formation', *Managment Science*, vol. XXIV (May).

Monopolies Commission (1968) *A Report on the Proposed Merger of Barclays Bank Ltd, Lloyds Bank Ltd and Martins Bank Ltd* (HMSO).

Morse, J. (1981) 'How British Banking has Changed', Stamp Memorial Lecture, University of London.

Morris, T. (1986) 'Union Competition and Merger in the Clearing Banks', *Industrial Relations Journal*, vol. 17, no. 2.

National Board for Prices and Incomes (1965) *Salaries of Midland Bank Staff*, Cmnd 2839 (HMSO).

——— (1969) *Pay in the London Clearing Banks*, Cmnd 3943 (HMSO).

National Union of Bank Employees (1965) *Pay Pattern for Banking*.

——— (1973) *Registration Under the Industrial Relations Act 1971: Why NUBE Registered.*

Nevin, E. and E. Davis (1970) *The London Clearing Banks* (Elek Books)

Nicholas, T. (1982) 'Effects on Retail Banking', *The Banks and Technology in the 1980s* (IOB)

Olson, M. (1976) 'The Political Economy of Comparative Growth Rates', *US Economic Growth from 1976 to 1986: Prospects, Problems and Patterns* (Studies for Congress of USA, vol. 2).

Pay Board (1974) *London Weighting*, Advisory Report no. t, Cmnd 5660 (HMSO).

Peters, T. and R. Waterman (1982) *In Search of Excellence* (Harper and Row: NY).

Pettigrew, A. (1985) *The Awakening Giant: Continuity and Change in ICI* (Blackwell).

Poole, M. and R. Mansfield (eds) (1980) *Managerial Role in Industrial Relations* (Gower).

Porter, M. (1980) *Competitive Strategy* (Free Press).

Povall, M. (1985) 'Women in Banking', in Livy, B. (ed.).

Povall, M. A. De Jong, M. Chalude *et al.* (1982) 'Banking on Women Managers', *Management Today* (February).

Prandy, K., A. Stewart and R.M. Blackburn (1982) *White Collar Work* (Macmillan).

——— (1983) *White Collar Unionism* (Macmillan).

Purcell, J. (1983) 'The Management of Industrial Relation in the Modern Corporation: Agenda for Research', *British Journal of Industrial Relations*, vol. XXI, no. 1.

Purcell, J. and R. Smith (1979) *The Control of Work* (Macmillan).

Purcell, J. and K. Sisson (1983) 'Strategies and Practice in the Management of Industrial Relations', in G.S. Bain (ed.).

Purcell, J. (1986) 'Corporate Personnel Departments and the Management of Industrial Relations: Two Case Studies in Ambiguity', *Journal of Management Studies* (March).

Rajan, A. (1984) *New Technology and Employment in the Financial Services Sector* (Gower).

Riseborough, P. (1982) 'Attitudes to Unionisation and the Industrial Relations System in a Clearing Bank' (PhD thesis, City University).

Roberts, B.C. *et al.* (1972) *Reluctant Militants* (Heinemann).

Robertson, J. *et al.* (1982) *Structure and Employment Prospects of the Service Industries*, Research Paper no. 30, Dept. of Employment.

Robinson, O. (1969) 'Representation of the White Collar Worker: the Bank Staff Associations in Britain', *British Journal of Industrial Relations*, vol. VII, no. 1.

Routh, G. (1980) *Occupation and Pay in Great Britain 1906–79* (Macmillan).

Rybczynski, T.M. (1984) 'The UK Financial System in Transition', *National Westminster Quarterly Review* (November).

Sayers, R.S. (1957) *Lloyds Bank in the History of English Banking* (OUP).

Shaw, E. and N. Coulbeck (1983) *UK Retail Banking Prospects in the Competitive 1980s* (Staniland Hall).

Sisson, K. (1983) 'Employers Organisations', in G.S. Bain (ed.).

Slichter, S., J. Healey and E. Livernash (1960) *The Impact of Collective Bargaining on Management* (Brookings).

Strauss, G. (1954) 'White Collar Unions are Different', *Harvard Business Review*, vol. 32 (September).

Strinati, D. (1982) *Capitalism, the State and Industrial Relations* (Croom Helm).

Swabe, A. and P. Price (1984) 'Building a Permanent Association: the Development of Staff Associations in the Building Societies', *British Journal of Industrial Relations*, vol. XXII, no. 2.

Thirlwall, A. (1982) 'Deindustrialisation in the United Kingdom', *Lloyds Bank Review*, no. 144.

Thomason, G. (1984) *A Textbook of Personnel Management* (IPM).

Thomson, A. and M. Warner (eds.) (1981) *The Behavioural Sciences and Industrial Relations* (Gower).

Thomson, A. (1983) 'The Context of Management Behaviour in Industrial Relations in the Public and Private Sectors', in Thurley and Wood (eds.).

Thurley, K. and S. Wood (1983) *Industrial Relations and Management Strategy* (CUP).

Timperley, S. (1980) 'Organisational Strategies and Industrial Relations', *Industrial Relations Journal*, vol. 11, no. 5.

Tuke, A. and R. Gillman (1972) *Barclays Bank Ltd. 1926–69* (Barclays Bank).

Turner, G. (1985) 'A New Strategy at Barclays', *Long Range Planning*, vol. 18, no. 3.

Turner, H.A. (1968) 'The Royal Commission's Research Papers', *British Journal of Industrial Relations*, vol. VI, no. 3.

Undy, R. *et al.* (1981) *Change in Trade Unions* (Hutchinson).

Vittas, D. and P. Frazer (1980) 'Competition in Retail Banking. (pts I & II), *The Banker* (Feb./March).

Vittas, D. and R. Brown (1982) *Bank Lending and Industrial Investment: A Response to Recent Criticisms* (BIS).

Wadsworth, J. (1973) *The Banks and the Monetary Systems in the UK. 1959–71* (Methuen).

Warner, M. (ed.) (1984) *Microprocessors, Manpower and Society* (Gower).

Weekes, B. *et al.* (1975) *Industrial Relations and the Limits of the Law* (Blackwell).

Willman, P. and R. Cowan (1984) 'New Technology in Banking: The Impact of Autotellers on Staff Numbers', in M. Warner (ed.).

Willman, P. and T. Morris (1985) 'Union Growth and Membership Diversification: The Case of the Banking Insurance and Finance Union', LBS (mimeo).

Willman, P. and G. Winch (1985) *Innovation and Management Control: Labour Relations at BL Cars* (CUP).

Wilson Committee Report (1981) *Report of the Committee to Review the Functioning of Financial Institutions*, Chairman: H. Wilson.

Winton, J. (1982) *Lloyds Bank 1918–69* (CUP).

Winterton, J. and R. Winterton (1982) 'Employee Representation in Building Societies', *Employee Relations*, vol. 4, no. 2.

INDEX

Page references in italics refer to Tables. (F) after a page number indicates a Figure.

Printed in the USA/Agawam, MA
May 31, 2012

566265.003